# Reading the Skull

While there are a handful of introductory texts and resources on 2D drawing for facial identification and reconstruction, most often they don't go beyond this cursory presentation of the subject. There is need for an advanced text available for artists who wish to learn more about reading and understanding the skull to inform more accurate and detailed 2D craniofacial reconstruction work.

*Reading the Skull: Advanced 2D Reconstruction* fills this need by providing instruction on how to identify basic features, as well as indicators and anomalies in bone structures, to help in illustrating more specific and unique details in facial structure and features. Since artists are most frequently visual learners, the book presents comparative photos of skulls with life photos to help better identify and decipher distinguishing facial characteristics. Because many forensic artists perform few reconstructions each year—and have very little exposure to skulls—the author has written this text to show examples of distinct elements in the skull for artists to see, compare, and learn. In doing so, it provides those who do not regularly work with skulls more exposure to them and allows readers the ability to apply such information and better extrapolate features for the purpose of more accurately rendering an individual's unique facial features. When examining the skull closely, each feature can be more detailed based on what the bone is indicating, and the work can be more accurate to that specific skull. Characteristics such as the ears, facial harmony and symmetry, shape of eye and brow, nose and mouth, the aging process, sex and ancestral background—among others—are all singular to that skull and adds to the gestalt of that face to make it more identifiable as an individual.

*Reading the Skull* is a ground-breaking collection of the author's personal study and research, other published works from the literature on facial features, as well as numerous examples from donors to forensic anthropology centers in the US. Work presented draws upon new information from anthropologists and others in related fields and disciplines who continue to study facial features based on the skull. As such, it provides a fresh perspective, summarizing several studies and work together in a single book.

**Natalie Murry** is a freelance forensic artist currently based in Austin, Texas. She began her forensic art career while working as a police officer in Kent Washington. She does reconstructions and postmortem drawings for the King County Medical Examiner's Office in Seattle Washington, and the Snohomish County Medical Examiner's Office in Everett Washington. She has taught forensic artists to draw digitally at workshops at police departments from Washington to New Jersey as well as at Scottsdale Artists School and at the Forensic Anthropology Center at Texas State University. Natalie is on the forensic art subcommittee for the International Association for Identification, and is an IAI certified forensic artist. She has had two articles published in the Journal of Forensic Identification: in September/October 2015 entitled "Rotating the Anterior View of a Skull into the Frankfort Horizontal Plane for Postmortem Drawings" and in April/June 2021 entitled "Skull to Photo Comparison for Identification Purposes." She has been a beta tester for Corel Painter since the 2016 build. Her work can be seen on her website, www.nataliemurry.com, on Instagram as @NatalieMurryForensicArt, and on Facebook as NatalieMurryForensicArt.

# Reading the Skull

## Advanced 2D Reconstruction

Natalie Murry

CRC Press is an imprint of the
Taylor & Francis Group, an **informa** business

First edition published 2024
by CRC Press
4 Park Square, Milton Park, Abingdon, Oxon, OX14 4RN

and by CRC Press
6000 Broken Sound Parkway NW, Suite 300, Boca Raton, FL 33487-2742

© 2024 Natalie Murry

CRC Press is an imprint of Informa UK Limited

The right of Natalie Murry to be identified as author of this work has been asserted in accordance with sections 77 and 78 of the Copyright, Designs and Patents Act 1988.

All rights reserved. No part of this book may be reprinted or reproduced or utilised in any form or by any electronic, mechanical, or other means, now known or hereafter invented, including photocopying and recording, or in any information storage or retrieval system, without permission in writing from the publishers.

For permission to photocopy or use material electronically from this work, access www.copyright.com or contact the Copyright Clearance Center, Inc. (CCC), 222 Rosewood Drive, Danvers, MA 01923, 978-750-8400. For works that are not available on CCC please contact mpkbookspermissions@tandf.co.uk

*Trademark notice*: Product or corporate names may be trademarks or registered trademarks, and are used only for identification and explanation without intent to infringe.

*British Library Cataloguing-in-Publication Data*
A catalogue record for this book is available from the British Library

ISBN: 9781032259109 (hbk)
ISBN: 9781032259093 (pbk)
ISBN: 9781003285588 (ebk)

DOI: 10.4324/9781003285588

Typeset in Myriad
by Newgen Publishing UK

# Dedication

**Figure 0.1** Dr. Kathy Taylor, aka KT. Photo by Barry Peterson, King County Medical Examiner's Office.

This book is dedicated to Dr. Katherine Taylor, former forensic anthropologist at King County Medical Examiner's Office in Seattle WA.

I was a police officer in Kent Washington when I attended a death investigation class back in 1999. KT was the instructor. She was so smart and so riveting that I had to talk with her afterwards. I told her I was going to a Forensic Facial Imaging course at Quantico to learn to portray the face of an unidentified person based on their skull, and asked if that would be something she could use at the King County Medical Examiner's Office. She was immediately positive and enthusiastic about the possibilities of another avenue to clear her unidentified cases, and that is where our friendship started.

The ME's office did not really have the money to pay for an artist back then, especially a new one with no experience. But I wanted the casework and KT wanted the images, so she would reimburse me by covering my parking at the ME's office and paying for my lunch. I assumed she used petty cash, but later realized she'd been paying me out of her own pocket. We learned over many lunches together that we both had gone to Mercer Island High School although I graduated two years earlier than she did. We talked about our cats and about the cases she gave me to work on. When I retired from Kent Police Department in 2002, KT was the only person from outside the department that I asked to my small retirement party. After my father died in 2005, we talked about our mothers being alone and their situations in life. We talked a lot about her fostering Jason and when she adopted Andrew, I went to the baby shower for him. She loved both of her boys so much. She was always a supportive and loyal friend, and I never questioned her sincerity or her trustworthiness.

As time went on, KT realized she may not be destined for a traditional family so she made her own work family out of smart women in the law enforcement community. She gathered around her investigators who shared her interest in her cases and wanted to work to solve them. One of my favorite memories was meeting at her house with others investigating cases and talking about different possibilities and avenues to explore to figure out what had happened or who the suspect was. We may not have met in person before that day, but most of us had heard of the others. KT brought us together. She and I spent countless hours on the phone discussing her cases and mine, even after I moved to Texas and started investigating cold cases. Whenever she would call or I would meet her at the ME's office, she'd greet me with an exuberant "Hi friend!". Even over the phone, I could see her big smile. She was excited to talk about a new case or developments of a present one. KT was brilliant in taking apart the information we had and using it to clarify the evidence that we may not have known we had. She never tired of talking about possible steps forward in a case and was an enthusiastic part of the investigation. The women she worked with became a group fiercely loyal to her personally and in work to a degree I have never seen with anyone else. Her joy was a gift.

When KT first fell ill from the cancer that would eventually take her, she spent time in a coma at Harborview. She told me later how surprised her mother was to see a steady stream of homicide investigators and law enforcement from local, state, and federal level come to her room to check on her. Even her mother was not aware of how important KT was to law enforcement in the state. She had always urged investigators and street cops to call or text her with any questions on cases. I personally called her when I was on patrol one day and had some bones that some kids in Kent had found, and I needed to know if they were human. She freely did this for everyone. She was a kind and important resource to law enforcement. Her passion was for identifying those who died without their name. She believed intensely that everyone has someone who misses them, and she wanted to bring that person home to their family.

KT was always willing to teach about her favorite subject: bones. When I was doing a forensic art reconstruction for KCME, I would go to the office and she would give me an area set aside to work on the skull. Her part of the case was to tell me the basics about the victim: the sex, ancestry, approximate age, and build. She went beyond this to teach me why she determined a case to be that way: to see things on the bone specific to that skull. I still think of the base of the nose in the way she said she taught it in her college classes: to consider if you were in a tiny car and going up from the mouth over the edge of the nasal cavity to get down inside the skull. In an Asian-derived skull, you would drive up, then across a little, then down into the skull. In an African-derived skull, you would drive up, then down into a ditch, then back up the other side of the ditch and down into the skull. In a European-derived skull, you would drive up to the nasal opening and tip over the edge and go down inside. It is a good visual picture that makes it easy to remember and I am sure she has many students that still think of it in that way. She would also teach me when I had questions about a specific feature on a skull that perhaps I had not seen before: a bump here or a divot there. She would tell me what it was and why it was, and I would have another bit of knowledge to add to what I knew about the skull.

After her coma and when she had been home a few months, I went back up to Washington to stay with her for a week and help her out at home. I helped with errands and chores, but she made it clear she did not want someone there to be a nurse as much as she wanted to learn. I showed her the basics of genetic genealogy, and we worked on her personal family tree. A couple of times, she called her mother to tell her of what we had discovered online. Even with what she was going through, her brilliant mind wanted to continue to learn. Whenever she forgot something, her ready excuse was: "Well I was in a coma ya know!"

Her friends built a shed in her back yard so she could continue to work from home, and I worked cases in KT's Bone Barn on a few trips to Seattle in her last year. She had investigators come to her home and sit in the fresh air of the back yard in her immune compromised state so she could examine the skulls and tell them information to help their cases. To me, they looked like students at the feet of the master who was still teaching.

She went into the hospital again a couple of days after I was at the Bone Barn for two cases in July 2021. I spoke with her friend Jean at KCME who told me it looked very serious, and I turned around and went back up to Seattle again to see her one more time. I stayed with one of my Kent PD friends who told me about one of her old homicide cases. A suspect who had recently been IDed in a case KT had been working for years in another county was now suddenly a suspect in this cold Kent case. At KT's bedside in the hospital, even though she was not conscious, I told her about this new development. I knew if she could, she would be so excited about this. She would think "so he did both of these. What else did he do?" and be going through the huge file cabinet in her mind to think of what other cases the suspect could have been involved in. The hunt consumed her, it was her life's work. We have lost a huge asset to law enforcement throughout the state. Some of us have lost much more than that with her passing. I dedicate this book to Dr. Katherine Taylor, as she taught me much of what I know about the skull and I miss her every day.

# Contents

| | | |
|---|---|---|
| **Acknowledgments** | | xi |
| **Chapter 1:** | Introduction | 3 |
| **Chapter 2:** | Photographing the Skull | 13 |
| **Chapter 3:** | The Face and Ears | 35 |
| **Chapter 4:** | Case Work | 55 |
| **Chapter 5:** | The Eye and Brow | 75 |
| **Chapter 6:** | The Nose | 103 |
| **Chapter 7:** | The Mouth | 139 |
| **Chapter 8:** | Facial Reconstruction in the UK<br>*Tim Widden* | 155 |

| | | |
|---|---|---|
| **Chapter 9:** | Traumatic Injury and Anomalies | 163 |
| **Chapter 10:** | Facial Comparison | 187 |
| Index | | 209 |

# Acknowledgments

Tim Widden for discussion about reconstructions and suggestions for scholarly articles. Thank you for contributing information about how reconstructions are done in the UK. www.timwidden.co.uk . Twitter: @timwidden

Dan Lamont for his vast photography knowledge and readiness to discuss proper techniques to a novice photographer. www.danlamont.com. Instagram: @danlamont_seattle

Ellie Nedell for assistance at FACTS photographing skulls. Your fast, accurate help and interest in the subject made the work go quicker, and I always enjoy talking about skulls and cases with you.

Trish King Stargel for sending me articles about specific features and your unwavering loyalty and support.

Dr. Daniel Marion Jr. for your friendship, support, and opinions discussing this subject over the past few years. I value your honest input and wry humor.

Jane Jorgensen at Snohomish County Medical Examiner's Office and Detective Jim Sharf at Snohomish County Sheriff's Office for their dedication to Cold Cases, success in identifications, and for allowing me participate in the process. Thank you, Jane, for all of your assistance in getting permission to use photos from my SCME cases.

Alan McRoberts for permission to reprint my articles that were originally published in the *Journal of Forensic Identification*.

Barry Peterson at King County Medical Examiner's Office for the use of your photo of KT and your friendship and assistance over the years.

Dr. Laura Fulginiti, forensic anthropologist. A close friend of Dr. Katherine Taylor, she has generously allowed me to ask her the questions that I used to ask KT about the skull.

Detective Jake Rodgers at Coeur d'Alene PD, Lieutenant Dan Smith at Olympia PD, Coroner Wayne Harris at Chelan County Coroner's Office, Coroner Dana Tucker at Cowlitz County Coroner's Office, Coroner Jeff Wallis at Kitsap County Coroner's Office, Cori McKean and Chief Deputy Coroner Ryan Gausman at Kittitas County Coroner's Office, Coroner Warren McLeod at Lewis County Coroner's Office, Chief Deputy Coroner Deborah D. Hollis at Skagit County Coroner's Office, Coroner Dan Bigelow at Wahkiakum County Coroner's Office, and Coroner Jim Curtis at Yakima County Coroner's Office for permission to use images from their cases.

Dr. Daniel Wescott and Sean Haynes at Forensic Anthropology Center at Texas State for access to the collection. www.txst.edu/anthropology/facts/ Specific thanks to the family of Thomas Meketa for allowing his full-face photo to be used in this publication.

Dr. Dawnie Steadman and Derek Boyd at Forensic Anthropology Center at University of Tennessee for access to the collection. https://fac.utk.edu

The directors and students at these facilities have been generous with access to their collections for my research. Profound thanks to the donors for their altruistic gifts to science and law enforcement.

# 1

# CHAPTER 1

# Introduction

I have been fortunate enough to have been able to work as a forensic artist since 1999. It is a small and specialized field, an uncommon type of art that is unfamiliar to many people. It is art with a purpose, and it is a privilege to be able to help law enforcement with their cases. Whether it is to aid in the identification of a suspect in a crime or to help determine the identity of someone who has died without ID on them so that their families can at last know what happened to their loved one, each case successfully closed is gratifying and humbling. To be able to help others by drawing is a rare gift to the artist.

It is a difficult field to enter, there are only an estimated fifty to one hundred full-time forensic artists in the US in 2023. Statistically few police departments employ a full-time forensic artist. There are some states that have none, while other departments in the country have forensic art units with more than one artist. Many forensic artists are police officers who do the work as a specialty of their employment, and thus only do cases as they come up in their own or neighboring agencies in between their regular duties. That is considered a part-time forensic artist. That is how I started. Often, they are trained only to do composite drawings, and not any of the other types of forensic work. Once they have taken the first week-long course to learn to draw composites, it is normally up to the individual officer to keep up the training and to seek out further instruction on their own. My department hosted composite training in 1999. It was the first workshop I took for forensic art and the first time in my life I tried to draw a realistic face although I had loved drawing since I could pick up a pencil. I continued with yearly composite training and then found out about the FBI's 3-week Forensic Facial Imaging course. I was fortunate to be able to attend that course at the

FBI Academy in Quantico Virginia in 2001. This course taught 2D and 3D facial reconstructions, postmortem imaging, and age progression to law enforcement only.

The training to enter the field is not standardized. Officers can request instruction by one of the forensic artists who teach, but the quality of the training varies with the teacher. Artists on the west coast typically get training from different instructors from artists on the east coast. Each artist finds their own training, so there is no one program where everyone learns the same skills or the same methods. There is presently no college degree in this field in the US. The only Master's program for forensic art is in Dundee, Scotland, and it focuses more on the British requirements than on the US-based types of work. If one is not in law enforcement, the choices are more restricted. Some forensic artists do teach civilians, but the prospective artist must find these courses on their own. Once they have training, it is not easy to get a job as a forensic artist if you are not already in law enforcement. Police departments usually do not have a budget for forensic art and civilian artists are not familiar with police procedure required to do the work. As I noted, there are very few full-time positions in the US; once an artist is hired in one, they tend to stay in it for their entire career. There are few openings for artists as a result, and many hopeful applicants.

Karen T. Taylor wrote "Forensic Art and Illustration," published by CRC Press in 2001. This was the first comprehensive book written about all the facets of forensic art. Caroline Wilkinson who started the Master's program in Dundee also wrote a book, "Forensic Facial Reconstruction" in 2004, published by Cambridge University Press. This book covered the British method of reconstructing a face from skeletal remains. Both books have been useful to me over the years when working cases, but I found them somewhat lacking as time passed. They are both excellent books that I recommend often to new artists, but the information about reconstruction is basic and limited.

When I first started doing 2D reconstructions from skeletal remains, I did only a case or two each year at most. With that kind of exposure, it was difficult to get a wide knowledge base about skulls from experience. I used the general instruction from the texts I had to find the standard location of the features, but I did not know to look at each skull as an individual. Each eye was centered in the orbital cavity, each brow followed the supraorbital rim, each mouth was six teeth wide. This did not consider the thickness, the roughness, or the shape of the bone in specific locations on the face. I saw each skull the same as the last one, differentiated only by sex or ancestry. The longer that I have been doing the work and the more cases that I have been involved in, the more I came to realize I wanted more specific details about how to interpret the clues on the skull to be more individual to each of them. I started collecting studies by forensic anthropologists, odontologists, plastic surgeons, and others in order to further my knowledge. I spoke with Dr. Kathy Taylor, the forensic anthropologist that I worked with regularly, and she was generous with her knowledge about the cranium and mandible. Whenever I had a question about an anomaly on a skull, I texted her a photo. She would tell me what it was and what caused it. The years went on and I continued to learn.

**Figure 1.1** Working on a case at Snohomish County Medical Examiner's Office.

In 2011, I started working with digital drawing software. I began with Photoshop, but transitioned to Corel Painter. I found working digitally made it much easier to make changes to my image. I was able to zoom in and out on the photo of the skull to see details that I could not see on the printed 8x10 photograph that I would be using if I drew the image with a pencil. Having the image prepared digitally meant that none of my shading would disappear when I put it through a copy machine, as I did not need to do that with a digital image. It was easy to email the detective a copy as soon as I had finished the drawing, and it reproduced perfectly for media and law enforcement bulletin releases every time. As this book shows, there are things you can do with digital work that you cannot do with pencil-drawn images. There is no difference in how the artist draws, however. The stylus is just another artist's tool like paint, charcoal, or pastels. The computer does not do the drawing for the artist.

**Figure 1.2** My digital drawing setup. I use a Wacom Cintiq drawing tablet attached to my pc and Corel Painter software. I also draw on an iPad using Procreate and ArtStudio Pro. Painter is the more robust program so I use it on all my reconstructions.

This book is intended to assist other forensic artists who want to do 2D reconstructions that are more detailed and based more precisely on the individual skull they are working with. It is commonly said that proportion is the most important factor in recognition. When doing a reconstruction, the proportions are already there on the skull for you, so you already have part of the drawing figured out. But every eye is not the same. It is not enough just to say the eye is centered in the orbital cavity and the eyebrow follows the superior rim of that cavity. When there is more information about the structure of an eyelid and the shape of an eyebrow that allows you to individualize your drawing based on that single skull, this can only help your reconstruction. Each feature can be more detailed based on what the bone is showing you, and the work can be more accurate to that specific skull. Every characteristic that is singular to that one skull adds to the gestalt of that face, making it more identifiable as an individual.

Artists are usually visual learners. For them, seeing something is easier to understand than reading a description of it. I have found previous information about features written in studies, but very few examples are shown in photographic form. It bothered me that something would specify a bone being average at a location or being thick. Many forensic artists in the US may do only one or two reconstructions a year, and this is an experience-based skill. If an artist does not have the experience with many skulls to know what constitutes average and what might be considered thick or heavier than average, the case suffers. I wanted to write a text that would show examples of each bone so that artists could see, compare, and learn.

At the beginning of each section in this book, I will give a short description of the basic information we have been working with regarding each feature. This description is highlighted by being in italic form. I will then present more detailed information that I have learned about that feature and show examples of how a bone shape affects what you draw, and additionally show a feature with different bone shapes in life photos. In this way I hope to give artists who do not regularly work with many skulls more exposure to many skulls. I want artists to be able to see and learn what to look for about each part of the face so that their work can become more accurate to each individual case. I would like artists to be able to refer to the book when faced with a specific bone structure, to see a similar structure illustrated, and then be able to replicate it for the skull they are working with.

Most of what I present is based on studies. Anthropologists and others continue to study specifics about the face on the skull, and new information is published every year. Sometimes studies are disproved, sometimes they are tested by others and expanded upon. This information is not provided to artists, they must go out and search for it themselves. I hope bringing several studies together in this book and showing what they mean will be useful for others. I have shown how some of these compare to what I see on cases from my own career and from donors to forensic anthropology centers in the US so that artists can judge for themselves whether they believe the information contained in the papers is valid to their work.

This book uses the medical terms for the bones and muscles. An artist needs to learn these terms to be taken seriously in this field. As a reminder, these are the anatomical terms of location.

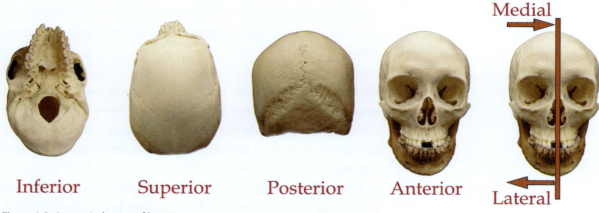

Figure 1.3 Anatomical terms of location.

Keep in mind also that when I refer to the left side of the face, it is on the right side of the photo and vice versa. That is easy to misunderstand if the artist is unfamiliar with discussing parts of the face in photographs.

Additionally, I use the terms "postmortem" and "antemortem" throughout the text. Most artists are familiar enough with postmortem to know it means after death, but not all are aware that antemortem refers to prior to death: when the person is alive.

While your forensic anthropologist will give you the general specifics about the skull (ancestry, sex, age, possibly size) I find it necessary to be able to examine the skull myself and see details that may not be important to the forensic anthropologist. If the individual is mixed race, the characteristics of the nasal opening could indicate one ancestry while the shape of the skull itself could indicate another. The skull itself could be male but perhaps the mandible shape is more typically female, or vice versa. All features should be drawn according to what the bone shows in that specific portion of the face or head while they blend together to form that individual face.

Regarding the life photos of the individuals: I was fortunate to have research access to the collections at Forensic Anthropology Center at Texas State and at University of Tennessee Anthropological Research Facility. I photographed many skulls that had accompanying life photographs of the donors at these facilities. The medical examiners in several counties in Washington State have also allowed me to use some of my casework from the many years I have been doing reconstructions for them. All these organizations requested I not show full face images of the victims and donors without permission. Any images using full face life photos are shown with permission from the forensic anthropology center, the medical examiner, or the victim's family. In some parts of this text, it is important to show the entire skull to illustrate a point. In some of these images, the skulls have had individualizing features or trauma changed or brushed out to make them less specific and more generalized. Those changes will not be to the feature being analyzed, but to other parts of the skull not specific to that area. Additionally, donors to the forensic anthropology centers often do not supply photos that are the most advantageous for forensic artist use. Most often they are candid photos not at ideal angles and with low resolution. Medical Examiners also do not always get clear anterior photographs of their victims when they are identified. I have used the best life photos that were available to me but I realize they are not optimal. Having access to them and being allowed to use them for teaching at all is a gift. I admire the generosity of the donors in allowing their remains to be used in research for science and law enforcement. Any additional sources of good clear photos to illustrate concepts are difficult to come by. Privacy reasons do not allow use of most driver's license or booking photos, which is normally what an artist gets when an ID is made. The quality of many of the images I am using is not optimal, but I have used the best I could find.

Some Medical Examiner's Offices were unable to get permission from families to use photos of identified persons from my cases, and I was not able to show those cases as I would have liked. I have instead shown my image from the case overlaid on the skull with no identifying information in the hopes that the comparison to the skull will be helpful.

I do not flatter myself that I know everything there is to know about the skull, but I have learned a good amount over the years. I hope to share it with you.

# 2

CHAPTER 2

# Photographing the Skull

*Previous texts have not given instruction in how to photograph a skull.*

Before an artist can begin to draw a reconstruction, they need photos of the skull to work from. Previous texts have not discussed photographing a skull in preparation for doing a reconstruction. Some medical examiner's offices have a photographer on staff that can take the photos, but most have not worked with an artist before and are unfamiliar with what images an artist needs to work with. I have always taken my own photos, but it has been a steep learning curve. My first cases were woefully poor-quality photos, distorted from the camera being placed too close to the skull and with no thought to shutter speed or focal length. I have asked a skilled photographer colleague to explain the best method for photographing a skull for a reconstruction, and his detailed instructions are included in this chapter.

## Materials

When I get a new case, I take the following kit of equipment to the ME's office.

In a small container:

Printouts of the locations where to glue tissue depth markers: the written description and the image of the skull (anterior and profile).
Printouts of tissue depth marker (TDM) charts for common ancestries.

Envelope with 3x5 cards and Sharpie pens.
Ink pen.
Spare TDM eraser sticks.
Small metal miter box with mm ruler glued inside.
Duco cement.
Box cutter.
Short metric ruler, as slender and bendy as possible.
Retractable tape measure.
Small package of tan Sculpey clay.
Long handled tweezers.
Ziplock bag of small foam pieces in various sizes.

Also:

Black velvet fabric, mine is 44 x 28".
Lazy Susan, 12" size.
Clear triangle with metric ruler taped to it.
Skull stand.
DSLR camera.
Tripod.

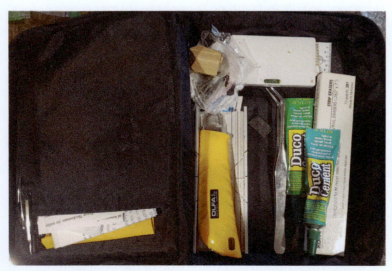

**Figure 2.1** My kit for reconstructions. This is opened, it zips closed. In the left-hand lid side in a pocket, I have printouts for reconstructions (where to glue the markers and charts for different ancestries), an envelope of blank 3x5 cards, and pens. In the other side, I have my miter box, box cutter, small rulers and tape measure, Duco cement, Sculpey, and tweezers. I also keep the Ziplock baggie of foam pieces here, so I have left a small bit of foam in the photo as a placeholder for the larger baggie.

I use the 3x5 cards to write the case number on, and then place it behind the standing triangle ruler so that it shows in photos. On the back of the card, I often write specific details about the case and/or the skull itself that I want to remember.

I bring the tissue depth marker sticks, miter box, and box cutter in case I had the wrong markers cut (wrong sex or ancestry), I need an extra marker, or the ME comes up with another case while I am there. I usually have a spare new tube of Duco cement.

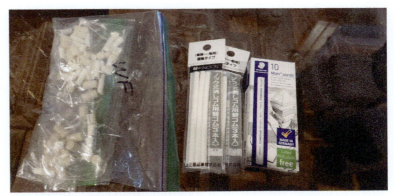

**Figure 2.2** I have the tissue depth markers that I have cut in advance according to the info provided by the forensic anthropologist, some extra markers, and some bits of foam which are also kept in a Ziplock. I have had to find different eraser sticks over the years as some are discontinued. These are the ones I currently use. The thinner Japanese ones are excellent for cutting the longer markers on the lower part of the face, they do not fall off as easily as the thicker heavier ones.

The Sculpey is tan in color and is used to replace the cartilage and disc at the head of the ramus, at the temporomandibular joint.

The foam that I use is what is normally used in Pelican cases or camera cases. It is polyethylene foam and you can buy it online. It is easy to rip it into various sizes as it is already pre-scored.

I bring the small rulers and the tape measure so I can measure to confirm the skull is in the Frankfort Horizontal Plane. The tape measure works best, mine is quite small.

The tweezers are just in case one of the markers falls off as I am gluing it and rolls into the orbital cavity or the cranium. I do not want to turn the skull upside down and shake it, but I am able to reach inside the skull with the tweezers.

I use the small foam pieces to get the skull into the Frankfort Horizontal. Often the skull will not be at the correct angle when it is on the stand, so I put little bits of foam under the cranium at the back to tip it up if required. They are also handy to hold the ramus of the mandible up in the proper configuration if the angle of the mandible necessitates it.

The fabric is required for a background. You can place it over some boxes or tape it to a wall, whatever works best in the situation you are working in. I find black to be best as the skull does not blend in to it in any way.

I place the skull stand and skull on the Lazy Susan. If the skull is difficult to set up in the Frankfort, I do not want to have to set it up again after I photograph the anterior and I need to turn it to profile. This is a great tool that I wish I had figured out earlier. Sometimes it takes ages to set the skull up perfectly for an anterior photo because it is in pieces or just doesn't fit the stand well, and the ability to turn it on the Lazy Susan saves having to do it all again for the profile.

**Figure 2.3** Folded black velvet fabric, Lazy Susan, triangle with metric ruler attached, and the rubber plumbing adapter that I use for a skull stand.

For a skull stand, I use a plumbing part. It is the Ferguson model 44U-305 flexible pipe fitting adapter. On their website, it is described as a 4 x 3 in. Schedule 40 Standard SV PVC Flexible Adapter. If I do not have this with me, I have also used a roll of packing tape as a stand in a pinch.

The triangle that I place next to the skull when photographing is taped to a metric ruler with packing tape. Leave a small space between both pieces when taping them together so it can fold 90 degrees and stand on the Lazy Susan. This type of metric ruler is called a framing square.

**Figure 2.4** Close up and angled photo to show the skull stand in greater detail. This is a heavy rubber material and this size is nearly perfect for most craniums to rest upon.

**Figure 2.5** This is how the triangle and framing square ruler are opened when placed next to the skull on the Lazy Susan or next to it. The two parts store flat but open out to stand, and a weight or block is behind the ruler to keep it open to the correct angle. The ruler should be parallel to the camera lens.

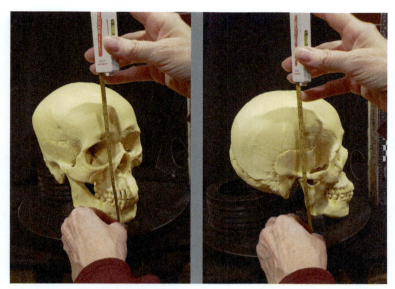

**Figure 2.6** The skull is placed on the stand and measured with the tape to place in the Frankfort Horizontal Plane. The inferior border of the orbital cavity should be the same height from the Lazy Susan base as the top of the external auditory meatus. A piece of foam can be placed at the gonion to hold the mandible up in the correct position.

This is the set up when I photograph the skull. The skull is on the stand with foam beneath the mandible to keep the ramus in the proper place, all of this is on the Lazy Susan with the black velvet fabric behind it. After taking the anterior photo, I rotate the stand so the skull is in profile, move the ruler to the middle of the facial plane, and photograph the skull again. I have learned over the years to photograph both profiles as there are differences between both sides of the cranium.

I asked my colleague, photographer Dan Lamont, to write out directions for artists to photograph skulls properly, as we have had no instruction on that in the US in the past. Some medical examiners offices have a photographer who will photograph the skull for you, but they do not know what information you are looking for from an artistic standpoint. They can certainly do the anterior and profile photos for you if you are unsure how to proceed and worried about distortion, but you should take additional photographs of the skull before the tissue depth

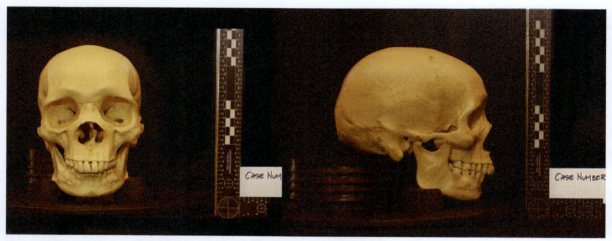

**Figure 2.7** Set up when photographing anterior and profile of the skull. Photos in these aspects are taken both before and after tissue depth markers are placed on the skull.

markers are placed on it. I will go into detail about additional photos following Dan's photography instructions.

# Photographing the Skull by Dan Lamont

To create a plausible, accurate likeness from measurements and photographs of the skull of a deceased person, a forensic artist needs to make photographs that replicate the human perception of "normal" perspective. Doing that right is all about the focal length of the camera lens.

Telephoto lenses typically cause "foreshortening" which makes elements in the image appear to be closer together than they actually are. Wide angle lenses do the opposite, stretching the perspective so elements appear farther apart (and sometimes distorted).

For accurate perspective the artist is best served by using a "normal lens." The actual focal length is determined by the geometry and physics of how lenses work. Without belaboring all that science and math (often not a happy place for artistic left brains), a "normal lens" has a focal length approximately equal to the diagonal of the image frame (i.e., the sensor onto which the image is projected by the lens and then recorded by the camera). Things get a bit complicated because not all cameras use the same size sensor. Luckily there are two sizes that dominate the market; so-called "full frame" sensors that are 24x36 mm and "APS-C" sensors that are 18x25mm.

Different camera makes and models have different size sensors. "Full frame" 36x24mm and APS-C 25x17mm are the typical sizes for DSLR and mirrorless cameras. All this stuff is in the manufacturers' camera manuals which, if the printed versions have gone missing, are available online. Or just look up your camera make/model and "sensor size" on Google.

Doing the math that means a true normal lens for a full frame sensor is 43.47mm and an APS-C is 30.8mm. Because of design traditions that you don't want to hear about, lens makers don't typically build to such odd specifications so the closest focal lengths typically available are 50mm (for full frame) and 28mm (for APS-C).

Often these days cameras are used with zoom lenses that incorporate many focal lengths. For correct perspective the artist should set the zoom lens at the correct "normal" focal length for the format to be used as noted above. To make the object (the skull) being photographed larger or smaller in the frame the artist then simply moves the camera closer or farther away.

Correct exposure is controlled by the size of the lens aperture (opening) through which light passes—the "F-stop"—to reach the sensor and the duration the camera shutter stays open (shutter speed). The F-stop is an inverse ratio so the bigger the number the smaller the hole (i.e., f2.8 lets in more light than f11, etc.). The shutter speed is a fractional inverse of the number displayed on the camera dial of screen so "30" = 1/30 of a second, "60" = 1/60th, etc. Almost all modern cameras allow you to set the camera on "aperture priority" and the shutter speed will adjust automatically to get a correct exposure. But there is one big caveat: the light meter controlling exposure in the camera by design assumes everything it looks at is of normal reflectance so if you are photographing a skull on a white background (brighter than normal) the camera may underexpose the scene while a black background may cause overexposure. Fortunately, with modern digital cameras we can check the image after it is made and either adjust manually as necessary or use the +/- exposure compensation controls that most cameras provide for auto exposures.

Another thing to consider is the depth of field, also known as depth of focus, which represents the range of sharpness from foreground to background in an image. Because of the way lenses bend light, using a bigger aperture (e.g., f2.8) will reduce the depth of field causing the point of focus to be sharp while the points in front of and behind will be significantly less sharp. If you use a smaller aperture (say f16) the object will be sharper from front to back of the image. Decide what you want to have sharply in focus and set the aperture accordingly.

Given the intended use of the photographs in the context of forensic art, most of the artist's photographs will require maximum depth of focus for best detail (e.g., smaller aperture and slower shutter speed) but if you want to emphasize a detail you can use a wider aperture, a faster shutter speed and a longer focal length to purposefully use "selective focus" to throw background and foreground out of focus.

Regarding point of focus, I usually try and make sure the nasal opening is in focus. That is on the facial plane, so I thought that was a good place to aim for. The details of the bone on that plane are the most important. In general, because of the physics of lenses it is best to place your primary point of focus about a third of the way into the scene to achieve the best depth of field.

Also, since you are creating life portraits from the skull you may want to make some photographs with a slightly telephoto "portrait lens" look which purposely uses a modestly longer focal length to slightly compress the perspective, which can help draw attention to the features of the face, etc. You might be familiar with Apple iPhones which now have this phenomenon replicated algorithmically in their so-called "portrait" setting.

Speaking of iPhone cameras, the image quality gets better all the time but while pretty amazing the images are not in "normal" perspective. The primary default setting for an iPhone is actually a pretty significant wide-angle lens so using an iPhone for forensic images will result in inaccurate perspective.

Finally, it is of course always best to use a tripod for these forensic photographs. This allows for careful framing and helps reduce the chances that camera movement at slow shutter speeds will throw the photographs out of focus. Dragging that tripod around can be a pain but it is worth it.

## Summary

To simplify some of that: my lens is an 18/70mm zoom lens. If I Google my camera make and model, it shows it has an APS-C sensor.

Cameras with an APS-C sensor should be set at about 30mm focal length.
Cameras with a fixed focal length (not a zoom lens) of 50mm stay on 50mm.
Cameras with a micro 4/3 should be set at about 25mm focal length.

These three constitute most consumer level camera lenses.

**Figure 2.8** My camera's sensor is an APS-C. That means the lens should be set at about 30mm for the image to be undistorted. The camera does not need to be a particular distance from the subject once this is set correctly.

Sony Alpha DSLR-A100

| | |
|---|---|
| Max resolution | 3872 x 2592 |
| Effective pixels | 10 megapixels |
| Sensor Size | APS-C (23.6 x 15.8 mm) |

# Taking all of your photographs

For many artists, you will only have one session with the skull. You need to make sure you have all the photographs that you will need for the future. It is better to have some that you will not use than to get a call a few years later with a question about the case, and not have a photo that shows that specific feature. Always take more than you think you will need. Photograph from all sides, including the superior and inferior views. If there is trauma to the skull, photograph the trauma.

Before putting on tissue depth markers, you should photograph the whole skull. Take closeups of areas that you think are individual to this skull: anomalies, abnormalities, large muscle attachments, a crooked feature, a heavy brow ridge, an uneven mandible.

# PHOTOGRAPHING THE SKULL 23

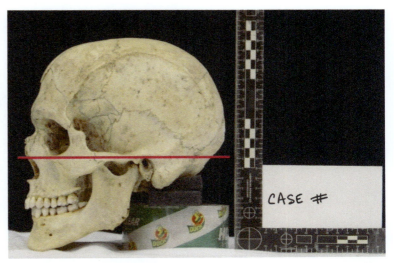

**Figure 2.9** Photograph the skull in the Frankfort Horizontal in profile. (This red line was added afterwards in digital software to show the FHP.) Photograph both profiles, right and left.

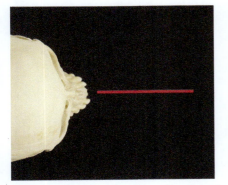

**Figure 2.10** Midline for the profile. Ruler is placed at the location of the red line.

Be sure the ruler is placed midline on the cranium when photographing the profile views.

Photograph the anterior view of the skull. In this aspect, the ruler is placed even with the facial plane.

Look at the orbital cavities. Check for sharpness of the superior edge, medially and laterally. Look to see if they are even in height on the skull or if one is lower than the other. Observe the lateral edge of the orbital cavity and see if the malar tubercle is visible or if you can find it by touch.

If the malar tubercle is absent, the eyelid will attach 8.5mm inferior to the frontozygomatic suture in males and 9.5mm in females.[1] Look at the shape of the orbital openings. Are they tall and open medially, or does the brow ridge descend and make the cavities look hooded or protected? The eyes will echo this. Look again at the superior edge of the orbital cavities, both medially and laterally. Note the thickness of the bone laterally, superior to the frontozygomatic suture. You are looking for clues to the eyebrow structure.

## 24    READING THE SKULL

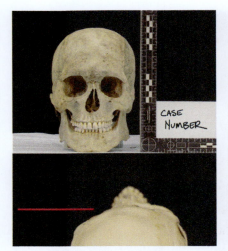

**Figure 2.11** Anterior view of skull. The red line in the bottom image shows placement of the ruler at the facial plane. Notice the asymmetry of the facial plane on this skull. The left side of the face slopes back sharply while the right side of the face is more forward-projecting. This is not something that is easy to portray in an anterior drawing, but it is good to keep in mind when looking for all anomalies on a face. It can tie in with other features that you can draw on an anterior drawing to help individualize the subject.

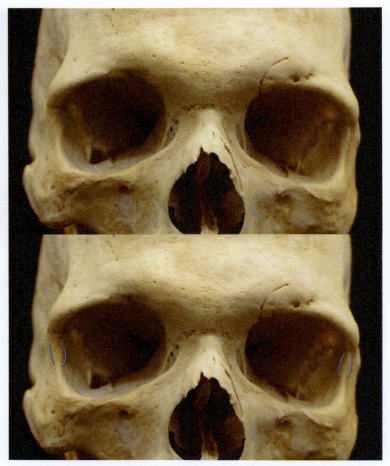

**Figure 2.12** Malar tubercles, also known as Whitnall's tubercle. This is where the eyelid attaches on the lateral edge of the orbital cavity. For some skulls, you cannot see the tubercles but you can feel them on the inside edge of the orbital cavity. Note how this skull's right orbital cavity is significantly higher than the left.

Photograph the nasal opening (the piriform aperture) at an angle.

The profile photo will show the angle of the nasal spine, but it is helpful to get further information about the nose with additional photos. Look for the details regarding the base of the piriform aperture and for the shape of the tip of the nasal spine. The spine could be blunt, pointed, or separated into two sides. Skulls that have been buried or left in the elements may have a broken nasal spine, but photograph what remains.

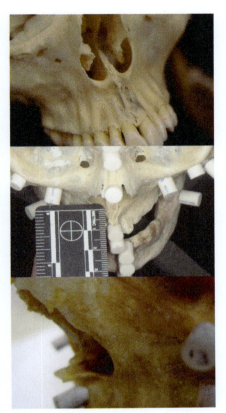

**Figure 2.13** Photographing the nasal spine at different angles. You are looking for the length of the spine and the shape of the tip, and observing the base of the nasal sill.

Measure with a small flexible ruler and record the length in millimeters of the nasal spine, tip to vomer. The vomer is where the two halves of the nasal spine fuse. If the two halves of the nasal spine are fused for the entire length and you cannot fit the ruler between them, just lay the ruler beside the spine and place the zero mark where you believe the vomer to be. Although the halves are fused, you can still see the structure of two separate sides, and there should be a place where the two come together. You can photograph this also if you are unsure, with the ruler held up along the spine. That may help when opening the image in digital software prior to drawing. You can zoom in to the photo and see if you can observe it any better close up. Any photos of the nasal spine are appreciated, with or without the ruler. You are looking to see the entirety of the spine to identify if it is intact and to see the shape of the end of it. This can be done before or after tissue depth markers are placed. A wide end to the spine indicates a thicker heavier nasal tip. A pointed end supports a thinner nose tip. A nasal spine that meanders side to side can indicate a nose that does the same. The length of the nasal spine is required when determining the nose shape via the Krogman method. If using other methods, this measurement is unnecessary.

Observe the shape of the entire nasal opening. Often, the two sides do not match. One side may be wider than the other, and the base of the opening may be uneven. One side may angle sharper than the other. Look at where the christa chonchalis inside the nose meet the edges of the nasal cavity. This is the height of the nostrils and may also be uneven.

Another useful view of the nasal cavity is looking from the inferior angle. I will discuss this 2011 study by Stephanie L. Davy-Jow et al.[2] in the nose chapter.

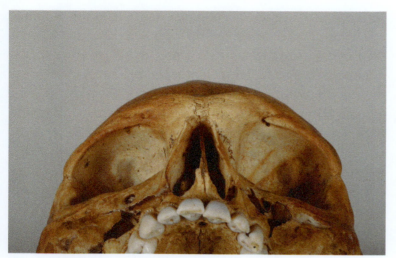

**Figure 2.14** Photograph the inferior view of the nasal cavity.

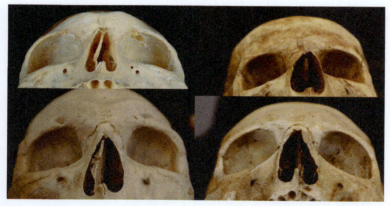

**Figure 2.15** In this view of the piriform aperture, more information can be determined about the shape and direction of the nose.

When you photograph the nasal opening in this view, more details about the nose emerge. In Figure 2.15, the top left image shows the nose leaning towards the left side of the face. In the top right, the same is happening. The width difference between both noses is clear. The nose in the top left shows the structure inside the nose is not straight vertically. In the bottom left image, the right nostril shows clearly more slender and lower than that on the left. In the bottom right image, it's opposite: the left nostril is lower than the right and the sides of the nose are not even. The left side of the body of the nose slopes at an angle, while the right side is more horizontal.

Look at the teeth. If they are missing, take a photo from an inferior view of maxillary teeth and superior view of mandibular teeth. An older skull or one where the person had dentures may have completely resorbed the teeth and there could be no indication of where they used to be. If there is an indication of at least some of the teeth, these photos will be helpful in size and placement of the mouth.

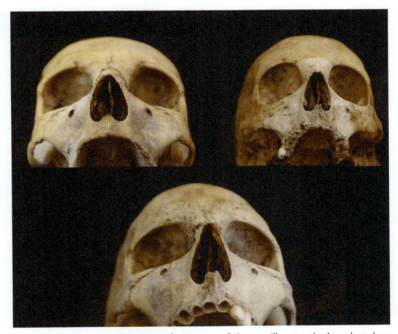

**Figure 2.16** Photographing the inferior view of the maxillary teeth. An edentulous skull (top left) may have little or no indication of where the teeth were. One with some antemortem tooth loss (top right) may still show where the roots of the teeth once were, depending on how long it has been since the teeth were lost prior to death. A skull with postmortem tooth loss (bottom) will clearly show where each tooth used to be.

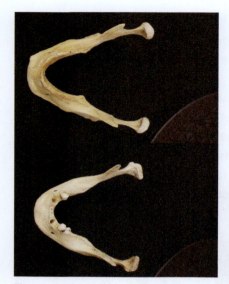

**Figure 2.17** Mandibles. The top image is edentulous, the bottom image has both antemortem and postmortem tooth loss. The postmortem tooth loss is indicated by the clean clear holes where the teeth used to be. The antemortem tooth loss consists of the incisors and molars. The bone has resorbed to different degrees for those teeth, depending on how long they were healing before death. On this skull, the incisors were gone before the canines.

Look at the roots of the teeth, the fossa above or below each tooth on the mandible and on the maxillary bone. Of most interest is the depth of the maxillary canine fossa. If it is clearly defined and deeply indicated on the cranium, the nasolabial fold will be prominent in all ages, although it gets stronger as the person gets older. If the skull is completely edentulous, there may still be indications of where the canine fossa were, and the width of the mouth can be inferred from that.

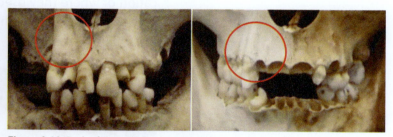

**Figure 2.18** Both of these skulls show prominent canine fossa to different degrees.

Take a photo of the inferior side of the cranium, showing the shape of the palate and zygomatic arches. The zygomatic bone and arches will give some indication of how to shade the face. Look at the nuchal crest to determine its prominence and thus the indication of a strong attachment for the trapezius muscle. The nuchal crest is also visible in the profile view of the skull.

PHOTOGRAPHING THE SKULL    29

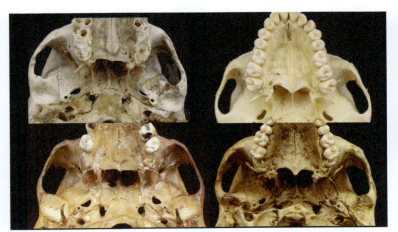

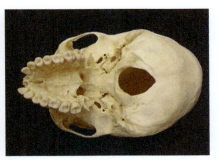

**Figure 2.19** Inferior view of cranium. Look at the shape of the palate and zygomatic arches. The nuchal crest is also visible in this view, if it is strong. This skull does not have a prominent nuchal crest. Skulls with prominent nuchal crests are shown in Figure 2.21.

**Figure 2.20** Zygomatic bones. Compare the shapes on these skulls, and consider how that would affect the facial plane. Top left has one rounded side and one angled back. Both arches flow softly away from the face. Bottom right is round and full. The top right and bottom left are both angled back, but note where the arch begins near the palate on the maxillary bone: the top right slopes back gently from that point where the bottom left skull turns more abruptly.

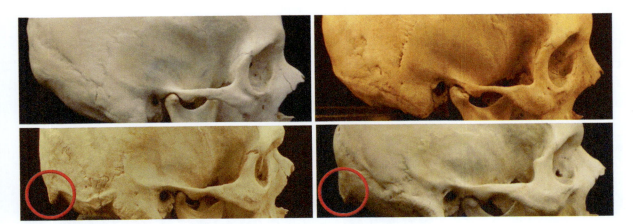

**Figure 2.21** The top images show negligible nuchal crests on the back of the skull. The bottom images show strong nuchal crests, almost like a ponytail, indicating they supported a heavy muscle. It is not necessary to photograph the nuchal crest separately, it is visible on the profile photos.

A superior view of the cranium will show the general shape of the head and any asymmetry to the facial plane.

Figure 2.23 Anterior view of mandible.

Figure 2.22 Superior views of the cranium. Notice the asymmetry to the facial plane on the middle and right craniums. The middle cranium also has asymmetry to the entire skull shape. It bulges out on the left side and is straighter on the right.

Photograph an anterior view of the mandible. Take a profile photo if there is anything unusual in that view, protuberances, or abnormalities. It is not necessarily a photo I would use in most cases, but it is best to have it and not need it than to not have it later when you no longer have access to the skull.

On the cranium, note the mastoid processes and make sure to check the direction they are pointing and if they are rough or smooth. See how much they stick out from the head and pay attention to the shape of the cranium above them.

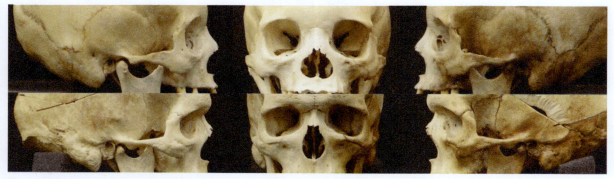

Figure 2.24 Mastoid processes, both sides of the head. Top skull shows smooth mastoid processes tucked in close to the cranium. In the bottom skull, the mastoid on the left side of the skull is rough but tucks in closer to the skull than the right side mastoid process. The right side comes down to a point and is smoother, but more substantial in the anterior view than the left.

That should give you a good selection of photographs to keep with the case file. You may not see the need for some of the photos right away, but it is possible to get a call about a case years later that could require extra views of the skull. It is not uncommon to be contacted by the case detective years after the reconstruction was done, asking for a comparison to a life photo of a missing individual. Life photos are often not straight anterior or profile angles, so the extra photos could be useful. Additionally, the possible individual may have a prominent feature on their face or head, or some asymmetry that you have documented in your photos.

## Notes

1 Fedosyutkin, Boris A. & Nainys, Jonas V. (1993) The Relationship of Skull Morphology to Facial Features. In Iscan, Mehmet Yasar & Helmer, Richard P. Eds. *Forensic Analysis of the Skull* (199-213) Wiley-Liss.

2 Davy-Jow, Stephanie, Decker, Summer J., Ford, Jonathan M. (2012) A simple method of nose tip shape validation for facial approximation. *Forensic Science International 214* (1-3), 208.e1-208.e3. https://sciencedirect.com.science/article/abs/pii/s0379073811003781

# 3

# CHAPTER 3

# The Face and Ears

*The face follows the tissue depth markers. Ears cannot be determined from the skull.*

When I originally received my training, we were told to just follow along the lateral edges of the tissue depth markers to find the form of the face. The markers in the midface would show generally where to shade the face. Ears were just a guess because they are cartilage, not bone, and thus no indications of them remain after death. As time passes, more studies have been done on the structure of the face and ears. We can now get more information from the bone regarding these features. It is believed that people do not pay much attention to ears unless they are unusual, but each small part of the head that is illustrated correctly adds to the overall resemblance of the individual in life.

## The ears

In 2009 Rynn et al.[1] referenced research in Russia that found the inferior border of the ear lobe corresponded to the mastoid shape. Thus if the mastoid shape is round and full, so is the lobe. If it comes to a point, the lobe does as well.

Stephan and Claes[2] say male ears are 4-5 mm larger than females and the ear is 6-8mm longer than the nose (not equal to the length of the nose, as previously taught). Ratio of ear breadth to height is approx. 0.6.

Additionally, for some years I have been examining my cases to see if they compare with Gerasimov's[3] statement that a downward-directed mastoid process indicated attached earlobes while a forward-facing mastoid process were indicative of free-hanging earlobes. Gerasimov also notes the protrusion of the ear itself goes along with a strongly developed mastoid process that bulges out laterally.

Wilkinson[4] says if the outer surface of the mastoid process is rough, the ear will show lower protrusion. If the supramastoid crest on the temporal bone is strongly developed and protrudes, then the ear will show upper protrusion (this is the area of bone directly superior to the external auditory meatus). If all these attributes are in place, then the ear has total protrusion. Massive prominent mastoids are characteristic of large spread-out ears.

I will illustrate these concepts with some photos of skulls with corresponding life photos.

THE FACE AND EARS    37

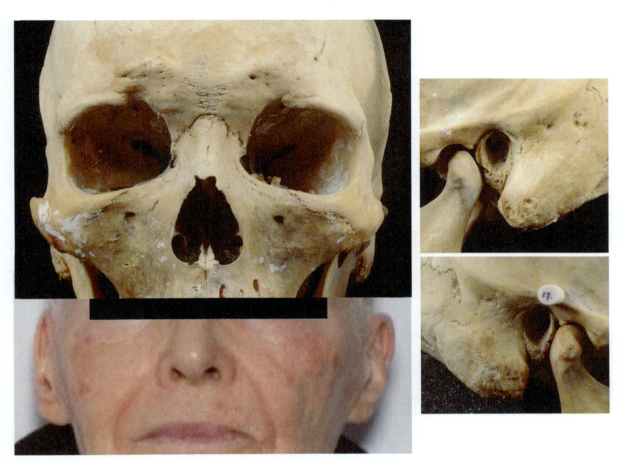

**Figure 3.1** Average ears

Figure 3.1 shows average ears. I have included mastoid processes from both sides of the head as the right ear has a different shape than the left. Notice the roughness of the mastoid process on the right ear compared to the left. There are more pits and knobs on the right side. The shape of the lower ear protrudes in a squarer configuration on the right as a result. These lobes are rounded like the inferior portion of the mastoid process.

The ears do not stick out very far. On the anterior skull photo, the mastoid processes are not prominent. In the life photo, the superior portion of the right ear is tight to the head while the left protrudes more. In my photos of this skull, both sides of the cranium flared out but not evenly. The outermost point of the flaring on the left was somewhat even with the superior edge of the orbital cavity. On the right, it was substantially higher. I believe that indicates the protrusion of the superior portion of the left ear was affected by the angle of the cranium, and thus that ear protrudes. The overall shape on the right side of the skull angles out above where the ear shape is involved and so the ear tucks in close to the skull inferior to the flare.

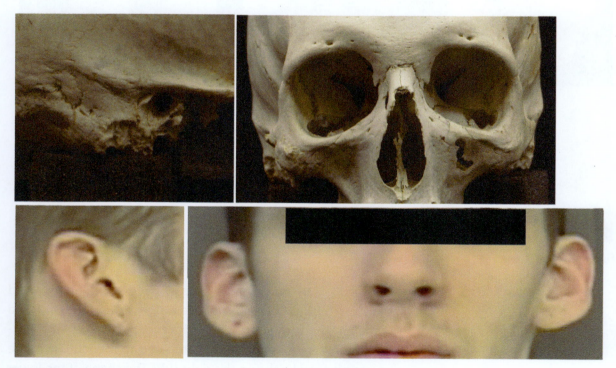

**Figure 3.2** Prominent ears.

Figure 3.2 This life photo shows ears that stick out substantially, and the ear itself has an unusual shape. In the anterior life photo, the helix of the ears drop straight down and then take a sharp 45 degree turn down to the lobe. The skull photo shows a strongly developed supramastoid crest – the skull comes out to a sharp point at that location (just above the external auditory meatus). The cranium is also substantially wider than the facial plane, making the ears jut out. The mastoid process on this skull was damaged postmortem, so I cannot address the shape of the lower lobe.

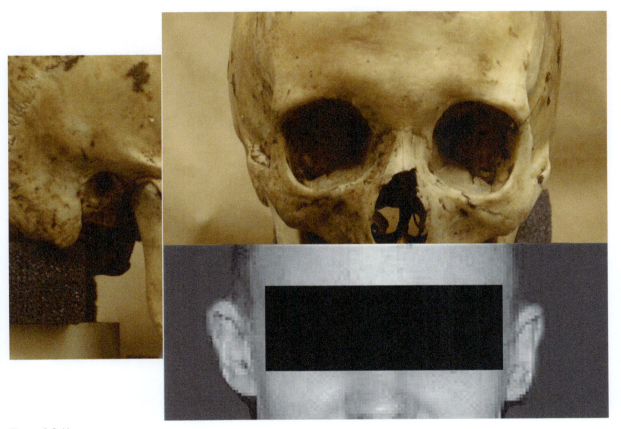

**Figure 3.3** Uneven ears.

The individual in Figure 3.3 shows the right ear jutting out further than the left one, and attached ear lobes. On the skull, the cranium juts out further at the right temporal bone, echoing that ear protuberance. It looks to have a fairly average curve on the left side. Per Gerasimov, attached earlobes should equate to a downward-directed mastoid process. The forward edge of the mastoid process does point downward on this skull. The lobes are rounded in shape.

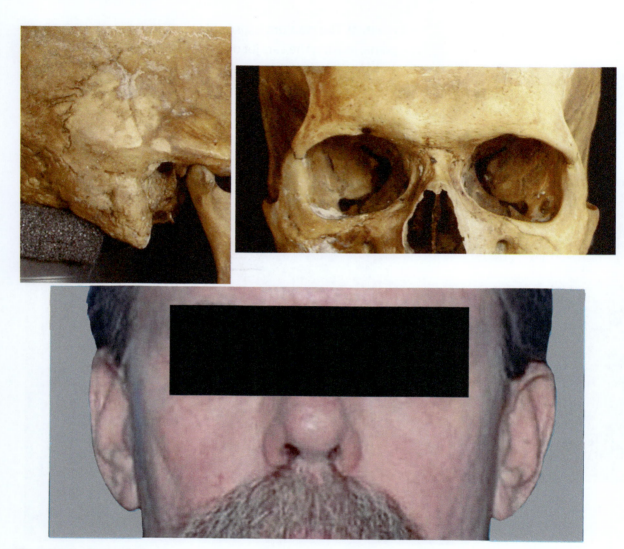

**Figure 3.4** Small pointed lobes.

In Figure 3.4, the ears are average in shape and size. In the life photo, the helix of the ear seems to drop down to a small pointed lobe. The skull photo shows a pointed mastoid process, also somewhat downward-directed. The cranium does not flare out at the temporal bones strongly and thus the ears do not protrude excessively.

# THE FACE AND EARS

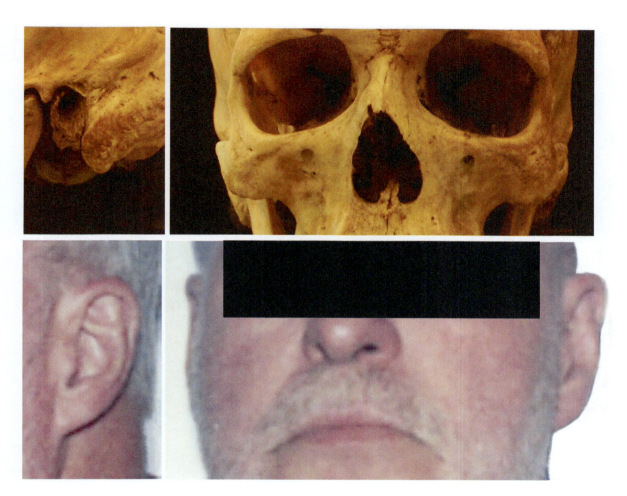

**Figure 3.5** Attached earlobes.

The individual in Figure 3.5 shows attached earlobes, and the ears are close to the head in the life photos. On the skull the mastoid process is small, downward-directed, and comes to a point; indicating a smaller attached lobe. On the anterior skull photo, the facial plane is not much thinner than the cranium itself, meaning the ears can tuck closely in to the head. I do not have a photo of this individual where the face is not at an angle.

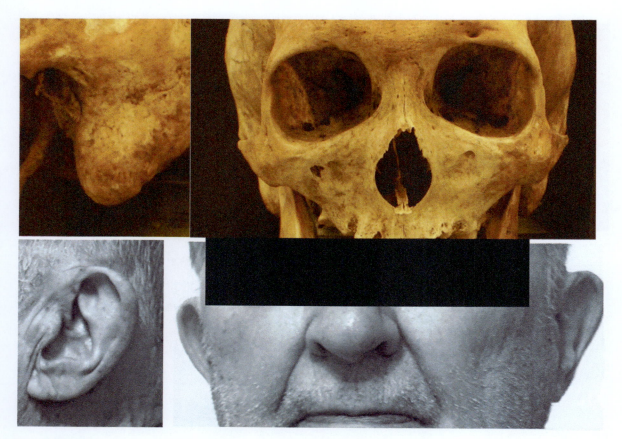

**Figure 3.6** Flaring ears.

The individual in Figure 3.6 has ears that flare out superiorly. His lobes are small and round. In the anterior skull photo, the cranium markedly flares in the temporal region – there is a pronounced change in direction for the top of the cranium. The mastoid processes however are tight to the head and rounded. In addition, they are downward-directed. The life photo profile shows an attached earlobe with a rounded form.

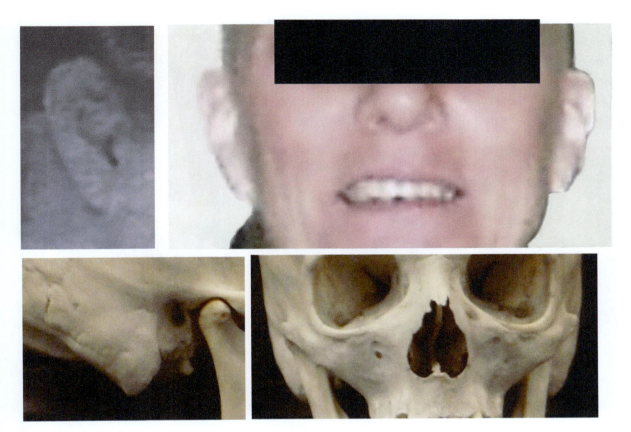

**Figure 3.7** Pointed lobe.

The individual in Figure 3.7 has average width ears that come down to a small attached lobe on the head. The mastoid process is downward-directed and comes to a point. The facial plane is not substantially thinner than the cranium, leading to ears that do not stick out but are not plastered to the head.

# Facial Harmony

A concept that is important in examining the face is facial harmony. I find that when you have one feature that is uneven on the face, often other features will interact with that one and follow the same path. The features are not islands unto themselves; they work together. That concept gives the face a singular gestalt, making it more personal and distinct from other faces. I believe it to be a key component of recognition of the face. Some faces have much more of this clear deviation than others and the artist must be careful in examination of the skull to find the subtle differences that may be there. I will illustrate these concepts in the next several photos.

**Figure 3.8** Facial harmony case 1.

In case 1, the face droops slightly on his right. This is visible when drawing a series of horizontal lines across the face at key points (the superior and inferior edges of the orbital cavity, the base of the nasal cavity, the base of the mandibular teeth, and the chin). Notice the mandible is lower on the right side of the chin, as is the general tooth pattern in the mandible. The mandibular canine in particular is lower on the right side, but that could be affected by the antemortem tooth loss of the left canine. Observe the shape of the nasal cavity: the right nostril is lower than the left and flares out further. The orbital cavity is slightly lower on the right at both the base and the supraorbital rim. Note as well the width of the cranium on the right compared to the left.

THE FACE AND EARS   **45**

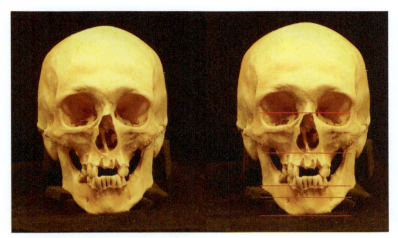

**Figure 3.9** Facial harmony case 2.

On case 2, this individual also has a tip down on the right side in the lower part of the face. The malar tubercle on the right eye is very slightly lower than on the left, but the nostril and mandibular teeth have a stronger dip to the right. The mandible is also lower on the right side across the chin. Looking at the skull without the overlay lines, the whole mouth region seems to bulge out on the right side. The maxillary teeth follow this pattern, the right side bulging wider and higher than those on the left. This then leads to the mandible flaring out on the lower left to compensate. You would want to examine this skull in profile to see the shape and protrusion of the mouth. Unfortunately the life photo I have of this individual shows him with a thick heavy mustache, so the mouth region is obscured.

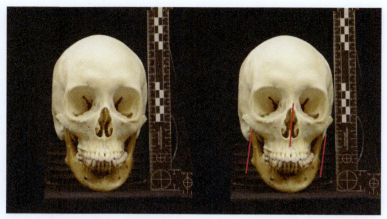

**Figure 3.10** Facial harmony case 3. Facial harmony can also be as simple as that shown in case 3, where the entire skull and features all show a long, graceful shape. The orbital cavities and nose are tall and slender, the skull follows this same shape. The nasal cavity swings to the right at the base. The face flares out to the right slightly in the mandible and cranium. She has a gonion flare on the right, but not on the left.

## Analyzing the skull

When an artist is inexperienced in analyzing the skull, it can be helpful to learn to see it closely using the following method.

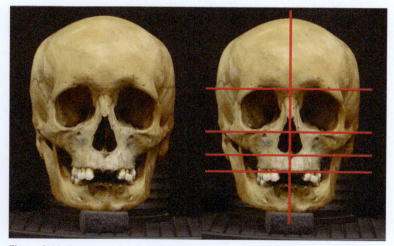

**Figure 3.11** Examining the skull. The anterior photo of the skull, and a second image showing vertical and horizontal guides (lines) at specific locations.

If using pencil, print out an anterior photo of the skull and use acetate to draw lines. If working digitally, view the rulers and guides on the image, and create a vertical guide (line) at the midline. Put horizontal guides at specific locations on the skull: the top and bottom of the orbital cavities, the base of the piriform aperture. If a skull shows obvious unevenness at other locations such as the mouth or chin, create guides there as well.

When drawing the vertical guide, I initially put it centered at the base of the piriform aperture and dissecting the maxillary line of the teeth between the central incisors.

Look at where the horizontal lines fall on the bone on either side of the midline. On the orbital cavity, one may show higher than the other. The line may be exactly at the base of the orbital cavity on one side, but be higher or lower than the orbital cavity on the other side. For the nasal opening, this will show if the base of the aperture is even. The vertical line helps to show if both sides of the opening of the piriform aperture are even.

If you have drawn a guideline somewhere on the maxillary or mandibular tooth line, this can show if the mouth rises or lowers on one side.

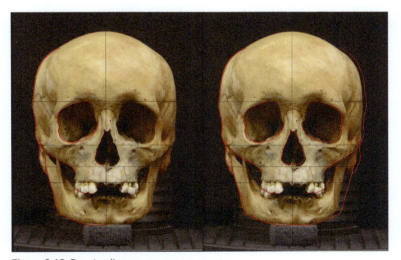

**Figure 3.12** Drawing lines to compare symmetry.

If drawing in pencil, use another piece of acetate. If drawing digitally, create a new layer. It is easier for this part to use a bright-colored pen to be able to see the lines more clearly.

From the midline, outline features on one side of the head. In Figure 3.12 on the left image, I have done the right side of the head. Follow along the edges of the orbital cavity, the piriform aperture, the side of the skull including the mastoid process, the zygomatic bone, some of the tooth forms if the skull has teeth, and the mandible. Take the lines all the way up to the midline at the mandible and piriform aperture. Duplicate that layer and flip it horizontally. Line it up so that the midline for the mandible meets with the first layer. This allows you to compare the structure of both sides of the face to each other. For the skull in this image, the left side of the face can be seen to be slightly lower than the right. The base of the orbital cavity, the piriform aperture, the zygomatic bone, and the maxillary teeth are lower on the left. The face also looks wider on the right, but be careful at this point to make sure your skull was photographed exactly straight on, and not with the camera slightly to one side or the other.

THE FACE AND EARS  49

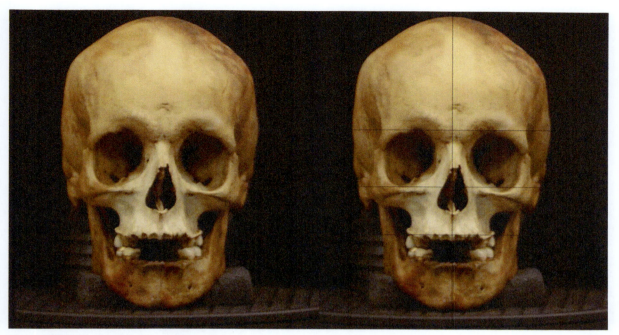

**Figure 3.13** Skull, and skull with guidelines drawn.

In a second example, initial casual observation can show the skull to appear fairly even. When guidelines are drawn, it is clear the left side orbital cavity drops significantly. The piriform aperture is even at the base, but can be seen to lean on the right side and the nostrils are not symmetrical. The base of the maxillary bone at the molars is higher on the right. The gonion is higher on the right.

# 50  READING THE SKULL

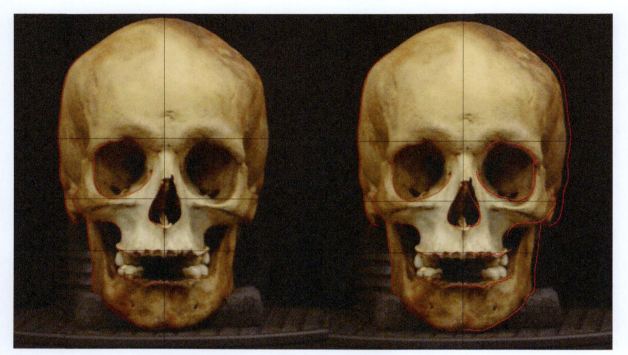

**Figure 3.14** Lines drawn around the features on the right and flipped to the left side for comparison.

When the features are outlined on the right side of the skull and flipped to the left, other differences become more obvious. Not only does the base of the orbital cavity droop, but the frontozygomatic suture on the lateral portion of the eye is also lower on the left. In this case, you would expect the Whitnall's Tubercle to also be lower on the left as it has a relationship with the suture. Compare the sharpness of the lateral edge of the frontal bone (at the temple) on both sides of the skull, and notice that the left side appears thicker and heavier. The lean on the piriform aperture is more obvious. The crease in the zygomatic bone where the muscles attach is lower on the left laterally.

In all cases, follow the bone.

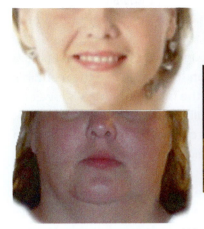

**Figure 3.15** Comparison of the mandible on both sides of this face. The difference can be seen in life photos at different ages of this individual.

For this individual, comparison shows the skull and mandible to be measurably wider on the left side. When viewing life photos of the individual, it can be clearly seen that this feature is seen on the facial level in life. The life photos show the individual at different weights, but the left side is clearly wider no matter how significant the weight change.

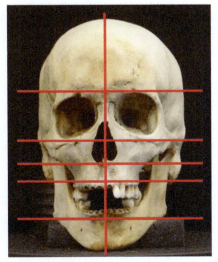

**Figure 3.16** Analysis of anterior photo of skull with a vertical guide at midline and horizontal guides above and below the orbital cavities, at the base of the piriform aperture, and above and below the mouth.

In Figure 3.16, even without flipping the features to check for asymmetry, it can be seen that the features all rise on the left side. The orbital cavity is higher, the piriform aperture and the zygomatic bone are higher, and the mouth rises up towards the left. The gonion is higher on the left, and the mandible angle is sharper. The mentalis is higher on the left also, so the mandible would be uneven. Interestingly, the mastoid process is lower on the left than on the right. The skull is clearly wider on the left, but I would want to check my photos or have access to the skull again to confirm this is completely straight on and not slightly angled.

When you learn to observe the skull closely to see this individuality, your drawing will be less generic and more specific to the person depicted. While it is advisable to stay ambiguous on things like eye and hair color and style, seeing what makes this skull different from all other skulls can only help in identification.

# Notes

1 Rynn, Christopher, Balueva, Tatiana and Veselovskaya, Elizaveta. (2012) *Relationships between the skull and face.* Wilkinson, C., & Rynn, C. (Eds.). *Craniofacial identification.* (193-202) Cambridge University Press.

2 Stephan, Carl & Claus, Peter (2016). Craniofacial Identification: Techniques of Facial Approximation and Craniofacial Superimposition. In Blau, Soren and Ubelaker, Douglas H. (Eds.), *Handbook of Forensic Anthropology and Archaeology* (402–415). Routledge.

3 Gerasimov, M. M. (1955). The reconstruction of the face from the basic structure of the skull. *Russia: Publisher Unknown.*

4 Wilkinson, Caroline. (2004) *Forensic Facial Reconstruction.* Cambridge University Press.

# 4

# CHAPTER 4

# Case Work

The following are some of my drawings along with the life photos of the identified individuals and some case information.

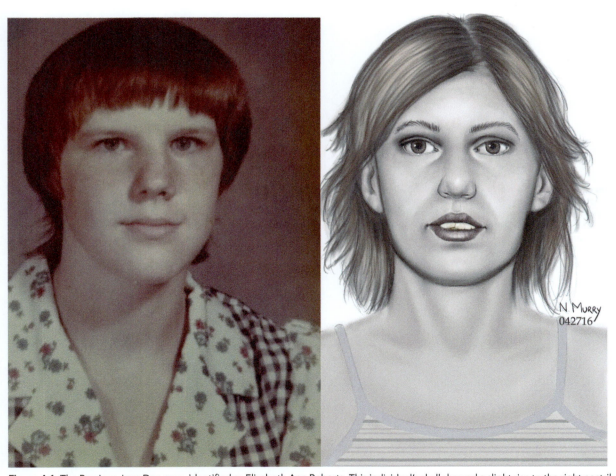

**Figure 4.1** The Precious Jane Doe case, identified as Elizabeth Ann Roberts. This individual's skull showed a slight rise to the right nostril. Her gonion was lower and more tucked in on the left, higher and more pronounced on the right. Her teeth were uneven, as the maxillary central incisors had been chipped in an accident and both tipped higher medially. Consequently, I chose to use her actual teeth in the reconstruction for recognition purposes. She had a deep dip to the bone between her maxillary central incisors, indicating a strong cupid's bow. Her mastoid processes were downward-directed. Her orbital cavities were not very large, which could result in her eyes appearing somewhat hooded in life, despite not having a thick brow ridge.

DOI: 10.4324/9781003285588-4

**Figure 4.2** The individual in this case was somewhat heavier than expected in this life photo and a little older than I drew him. None of the photos I was given were ideal for comparison purposes. His features were mostly even, although his left orbital cavity dipped down slightly laterally. The most unusual feature on this skull was the uneven mandible. The angle on his left side was much steeper than that on his right. That is visible in the life photos as well. He was found in hiking gear which included a red button down shirt. He was identified as Richard Arneson.

CASE WORK  57

**Figure 4.3** The skull for this individual had been exposed to the elements for several months, resulting in some breakage and complete postmortem tooth loss. I did not have access to this skull. The ME's office attached the tissue depth markers and photographed the skull, mailing me the results. This is not optimal. Examining the skull in person is always a better way to work. I was unable to see where the teeth had been on the skull because the inferior edge of the maxilla was worn down, so I had an investigator at the ME's office mark on the maxilla where the teeth would have been. The labeled photo indicated the width of the mouth to be less than that of the piriform aperture, which would be unheard of. I did draw the mouth very small as a result, but that does not appear to be correct in the life photo. If I had known at the time to check the infraorbital foramen that would probably have been more accurate. The piriform aperture was mainly even, just slightly higher on the right, but the crista chonchalis are even. The nasal spine has a curve and points to his left. It would be interesting to know if that has anything to do with the nostrils pointing in different directions. The mandible was uneven, with the gonion higher and wider on his left. The mastoid processes were ambiguous in what direction they pointed. This individual was identified as David McGhee.

**Figure 4.4** This is a case where I show how much difference the hair can make to an image. The first image is my reconstruction as released. The second image is the same drawing with the victim's hair superimposed onto it. The skull was notably wider on his right than the left. The bone flowed down more horizontally on his right side from his nose, and went out more vertically on the left side. You can see that in the way the flesh flows on his face in the life photo, the left cheek is fuller and slightly higher than the right. The right side of his piriform aperture was wider than the left and the left was higher. The entire nasal opening had a curve to it. He had a strong brow ridge and rough zygomatic bones. His mastoid processes were downward-directed and tucked in close on the skull. He had a very defined nuchal crest. These indications on the skull were that this was a stocky individual. This individual was identified as Shaun Moore.

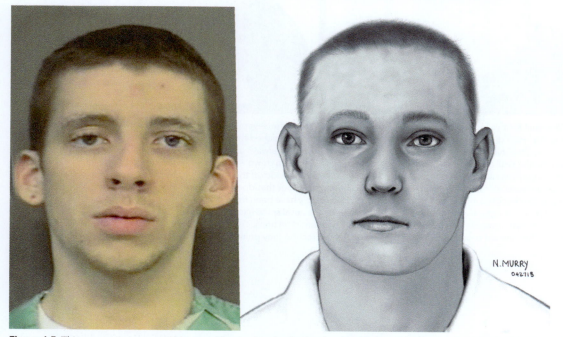

**Figure 4.5** This was a missing mandible case. The cranium had a slender nose and only two molars left in it, so there was very little info about the mouth. I did see that the central incisors would have been off center, pushing the entire mouth to the right. The orbital cavities were fairly high and rounded, the brow ridge was negligible. The zygomatic bones were very rough. The mastoid processes were damaged but the cranium flared out to a point at the occipital region, indicating the upper part of the ears were prominent. The forehead was wide and flat. This individual was identified as Tyler Sullivan.

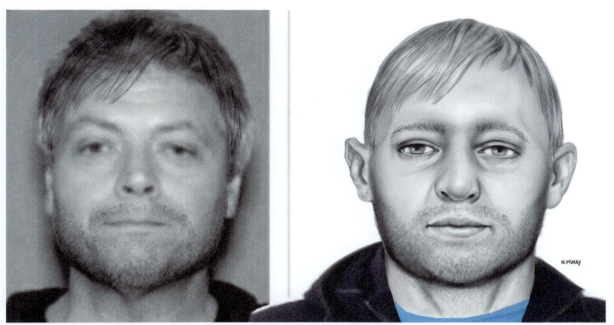

**Figure 4.6** This cranium flared out on the left side of this skull substantially. The individual had a strong brow ridge. The nasal opening was clearly lower and thinner on the left side. I knew to give him lighter hair as he did have a hair sample when he was found. I have overlaid the hair and the facial hair from my digital image to his life photo to compare with what I drew on the reconstruction. I did this drawing before I learned how to interpret the shape of the eyebrows and ears from the skull. This individual was identified as Timothy Conrad.

**Figure 4.7** This individual had a strong brow ridge. The lateral supraorbital rim on his right dipped down lower than on his left. His nose was quite slender and even on both sides. I drew this case before I read the studies about brows, but this skull had thickened lateral supraorbital rims. Those, combined with the strong brow ridge, would form a triangular-shaped eyebrow as indicated on the life photos. This is one of the cases where some time after I did the reconstruction I was presented with life photos of this individual, Horace Prescott, and asked for my opinion on if the skull was his. I did a skull to face comparison for the ME's office on this case.

**Figure 4.8** This skull was edentulous. I drew two versions, one edentulous and one with what he would look like with dentures as it was unknown if he wore them. The orbital cavities dipped down on the right on this skull, and he had a heavy brow ridge. The left side of the glabella had a strong angular formation and both sides came together at the nasion in a dual-knobbed configuration. The top of the nose tipped to the right. His zygomatic bones were rough and he had a strong nuchal crest. His chin was wide. This skull had smoothed with age, but I drew the strong nasolabial folds due to the age the forensic anthropologist advised, not because of indications on the canine fossa. The bags under the eyes, the drooping skin over the eyelids, and the looser skin on the mandible were also drawn to be age-appropriate. This individual was identified as Robert Jones.

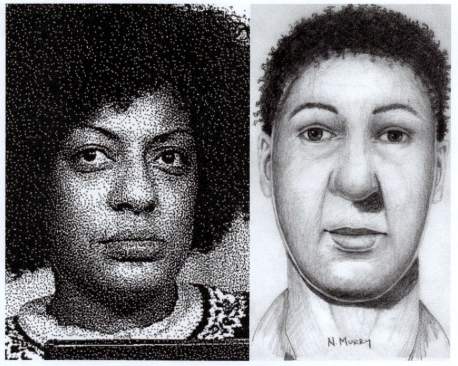

**Figure 4.9** I did this case early in my career and I know I did not photograph the skull properly. I also did not take enough photos. This was a challenging skull to photograph, as the individual had a dental plate for the maxillary teeth. The plate did not fit easily on the bone. The skull looked quite long and fairly slender to me, but I think now that was a result of my poor photography skills. Her piriform aperture was wider on her right but the rest of her face seemed mainly symmetrical. However poor I think the drawing is now, it did the job when a detective saw it and thought it resembled a missing woman case he was working. Upon further investigation, the woman was identified as Rita Lang.

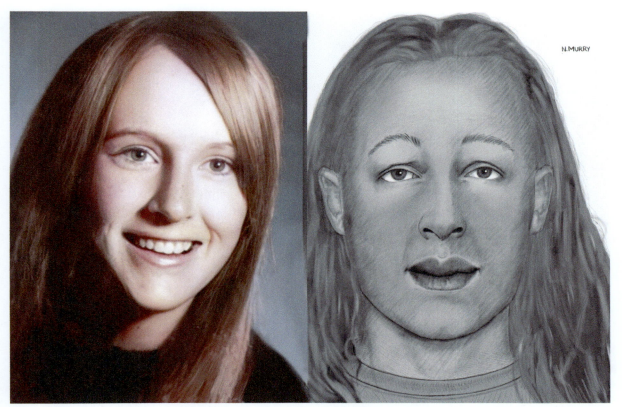

**Figure 4.10** This was the first digital reconstruction I did back in 2010. The cranium was somewhat damaged from being buried for nearly 40 years. Her orbital cavities were high and her nose was slender and even. Her mandible flared slightly to the right although her zygomatic bone on the left was thicker and lower. In 2010 I was still drawing the eyebrows along the edge of the orbital cavity, which made them too high as seen in this image. I have learned to drop them down inside the orbital cavity, at least medially. Her supraorbital rims tipped down laterally and I thought that might indicate a fold over her eyelid, which I have drawn on her right eye somewhat ambiguously. When in doubt, draw ambiguously. Her canine fossa were somewhat defined, so I drew a nasolabial fold. Her maxillary central incisors were tall. I do not have a life photo of her without a smile to compare the fullness of the lips that I drew. This individual was identified as Kerry Hardy May. Several articles call her Kerry May Hardy.

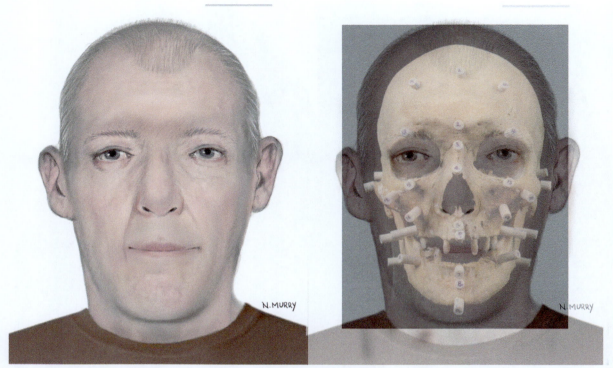

**Figure 4.11** The skull of this elderly man was mostly smooth. He had a strong brow ridge. His zygomatic bones were somewhat flattened and forward-facing. His piriform aperture was even and level. His canine fossa were not particularly defined, but I drew nasolabial folds because of his age. There are very slight points somewhat widely spaced on his chin. I did not draw them defined, but it appears they looked defined in life. He also turned out to be a little older than I pictured him, so even more loosening up of the jawline would have been appropriate. When I was drawing the image, the face felt somewhat Scandinavian to me so I gave him blue eyes and light skin. I was pleased and surprised to find that he appeared that way in life as well. The ME on this case requested I not show his life photo.

CASE WORK 63

**Figure 4.12** This was a very heavy skull with a heavy brow ridge and strong nuchal crest. The piriform aperture appeared slender with a blunt nasal spine. The face appeared wide and flat with forward facing zygomatic bones. The upper gumline was flat and all incisors were missing. It rose to the left. The malar tubercle on the right eye was lower than that on the left. The right nostril was higher and wider than the left. The mandible was wide with a gonion flare on the right. I did not see a huge resemblance between my drawing and the victim, but the family believed it was him when they saw my image. The life photo does show the right eye attaching laterally lower than the left, and the right nostril wider than the left. He also seems to have the tip to his mouth that the teeth indicated, rising slightly higher on his left. This individual was identified as Gerald Armstrong.

## Additional Cases

The following are some of my other cases that have yet to be identified, along with case information and the names of the agencies handling the cases.

# 64 READING THE SKULL

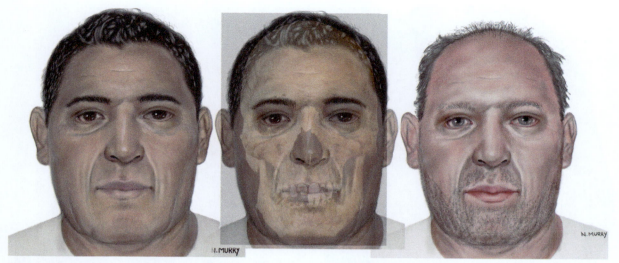

**Figure 4.13a** For this case, the forensic anthropologist went back and forth on whether this skull was from a Hispanic or European-derived male 40-60 years of age. The remains had been out in the elements for at least ten years. The ME asked for two different images, one Hispanic and one European.

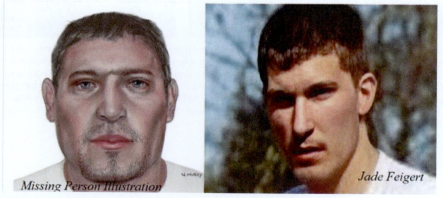

**Figure 4.13b** We eventually went with this image, a younger European version than the original. This is the ID photo provided from Monica Feigert from her Facebook page, Justice for Jade Feigert.

These remains were found near a Weyerhaeuser shipping dock on the Columbia River and had been there at least ten years. No clothing or property were recovered from the scene. This case is through Cowlitz County Coroner in Washington State.

The skull presented with some postmortem tooth loss and a broken central maxillary incisor, so I did not show the teeth in the rendering. It was robust with a strong brow ridge that had large rounded bone formations at the glabella. The right eye was slightly lower than the left. The nose looked fairly even at the base but flared out slightly on the right side. The body of the nose drifted right. The right zygomatic bone was lower than the left. The mandible was substantial with a wide chin defined by clear nodules at each end. The mandible appears to drop on the right side. Mastoid processes were somewhat forward-facing. The nuchal crest was negligible.

As this book was going to print, I received a Facebook message from Monica Feigert that this subject was identified as her son Jade Feigert through genetic genealogy. This is a reminder that I don't always get notified by the agency when the case is resolved, the artist is not at the top of the investigator's list of priorities when working the case. I'm grateful for Monica reaching out to me in her grief to inform me of this development.

**Figure 4.14** This is a missing mandible case. The forensic anthropologist described this individual as Native or European. His short occipital shelf, wide interocular space, and flat cheekbones pointed to Asian/Native ancestry. The age range given was wide: 30 to 70. He was 5'01" to 5'07". He had a strong brow ridge with a wide nose. The nasal sill is dull. He was wearing a red checked shirt and the waistband on his pants was 32/34.

The remains were found in mudflats north of Everett WA in January 1979. He had been there for months. It's likely he washed down through the Puget Sound to the confluence of Steamboat and Union sloughs. No identification remained in his wallet. This case is through Snohomish County Medical Examiner's Office.

The skull showed an average brow ridge. His supraorbital rims are sharp laterally. His left nostril is lower and a bit thinner than the right. His nasal spine was broken but the remaining portion was angled downwards. As he is missing one of his maxillary central incisors and all of his mandible, I did not draw him with an open mouth.

He had a fractured left femur that had healed without being repaired. This resulted in his left leg being 2 inches shorter than his right. That info is not necessary for the reconstruction but is good for the media release, at it would have been a defining aspect of his appearance.

As this book was going to print, this subject has been identified as Gary Lee Haynie. I do not have a life photo of him as an adult.

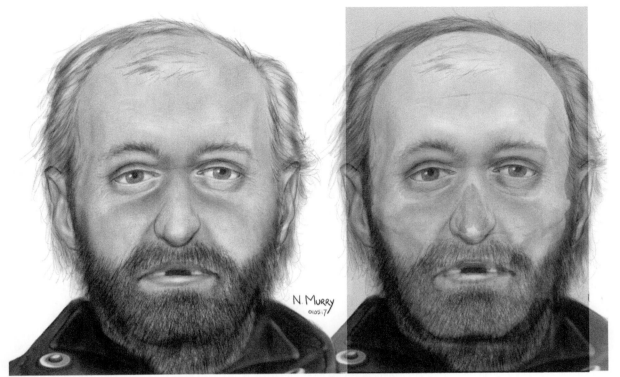

**Figure 4.15** This was believed to be a homeless individual, a European-derived male 40 to 60 yoa. He was found in Hawley Cove Park in Bremerton, Kitsap County WA. in August 2016. He was found partially in the water. There were no belongings or clothes nearby. This case is through Kitsap County Coroner.

His left orbital cavity was higher than his right, as was the left zygomatic bone and the left nostril. He had antemortem maxillary central incisor loss, so I drew him with a slight open mouth so that would be visible as it would have been something people noticed about him. The nasal spine was fairly long and pointed down. The mastoid processes tucked in close to the head and were forward-facing. Nuchal crest was negligible. The right canine fossa in particular was prominent.

As this book was going to print, I was advised this individual was identified from my drawing as Daniel Robert Bomberry. I do not have a photo of him.

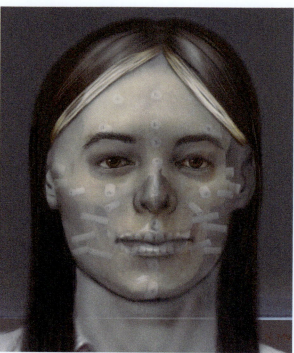

**Figure 4.16** This individual was described as a Native American Female 20 to 40 yoa and 5′ tall. Her clothing was petite. This individual was found in February 1988 in Union Gap WA along the Yakima River. The remains had been there between 4 and 10 months. She was wearing lavender pants and a long sleeved shirt with a Mexican label and brown bowling shoes. One shoe had a white sole, the other had a black sole. This case is through Yakima County Coroner.

The skull was in excellent condition and she had full dentition. The left orbital cavity was lower than the right and appeared to droop laterally. Malar tubercles were 15mm inferior to the suture. The piriform aperture was even with a flat sill. The maxillary bone and teeth indicate a slight Cupid's bow and full lips. The skull was somewhat masculine with a small brow ridge, a defined nuchal crest, and somewhat square mandible angle in the profile. The chin looked fairly pointed.

CASE WORK **69**

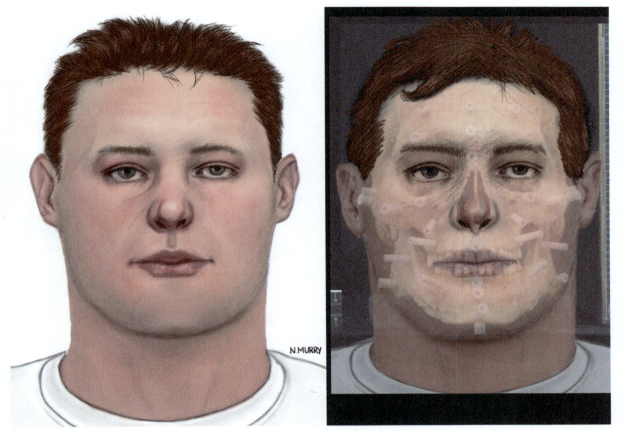

**Figure 4.17** This individual was found in a campsite off Sultan Basin Road near Sultan WA and was believed to have been there for one to five years before being found. He was described as a European-derived male 20 to 50 yoa, unknown height and weight. This case is through Snohomish County Medical Examiner's Office.

The skull was large and had full dentals. He had a small nuchal crest and average brow ridge. The piriform aperture was lower on the right side. He had a gonion flare, resulting in a wide mandible. His mastoid processes tucked in closely. The one on the right was smaller and pointed downward while the left one looked more forward-facing. DNA results said he had lighter-colored eyes: green, brown, or hazel. DNA also advised he had ties to Amish or Mennonite communities as well as roots in Texas and Louisiana.

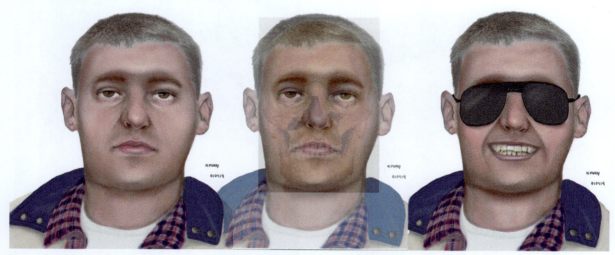

**Figure 4.18** This was a case that was photographed for me, and the photos emailed to me for the reconstruction.

This individual was advised to be a European-derived male 20 to 40 yoa and 5'04" to 5'06" tall. He had light brown hair up to 5 cm long. The ME provided photos of clothing, including a jacket and plastic sunglasses that I included in one version of the drawing. He was found in 1989 north of Burlington WA and had been there for up to 9 months. This case is through Skagit County Coroner.

The left orbital cavity is higher on this skull, but the left nostril is lower than the right. There is midface damage, but the zygomatic bones look even. The gonial angles are pronounced bilaterally. The medical examiner who sent me case notes with the photos noted the robusticity of the muscle attachments for the temporalis muscles, along the zygomatic bone, and underneath the oblique line of the mandible. They also noted the pointy asymmetrical chin. The mastoid processes were rounded and forward facing. The cranium flowed gently up from the mastoid processes, not indicating any particular protuberance of the ears.

CASE WORK 71

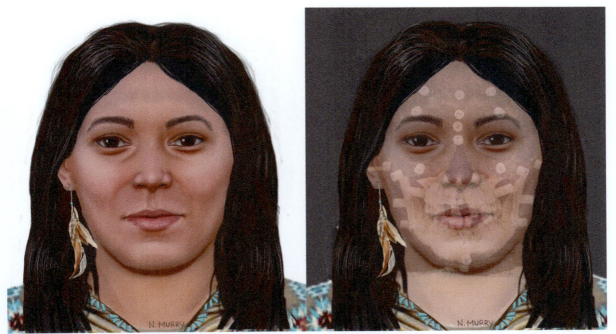

**Figure 4.19** This individual was killed in a vehicle collision in May 1991 on I-5 near Kalama WA. She had been riding in a semi with a trucker who had been on the road from Missouri. He'd driven through Kansas, Colorado, Wyoming, Utah, Idaho and Oregon before arriving in Washington on May 14. The unidentified female could have been picked up any time along the drive. The semi rear ended another vehicle on I-5 shortly after leaving a rest stop and burst into flames.

This individual was just over 5' tall and in her early 20s. She had been seen at the rest stop and described as a Native American with long black hair and wearing a feather earring. She had a severe curvature in her spine. This individual is known as Helen Doe, as the collision occurred close to Mt. St. Helens. This case is through Cowlitz County Coroner.

The skull was damaged in the fire and there was postmortem tooth loss. Most of her features were even although the top of her nose leaned toward her left eye a little and the right nostril was slightly higher than the left. Her mandible was even on both sides. Her cranium and mastoid processes seemed somewhat wider than her mandible, but that could have been from the damage from the fire. Her mastoid processes were rounded and appeared downward-directed. Her profile showed a low nasal bridge and her zygomatic bones were flat.

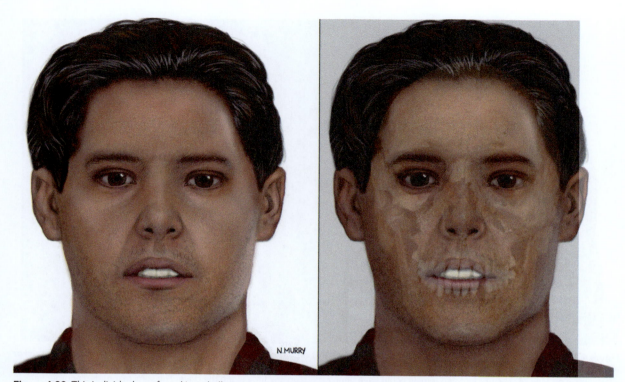

**Figure 4.20** This individual was found in a shallow grave in the 200 block of 130th St. NE in South Everett WA in September 2020. He was described as male 22-43 yoa and of Native American, Asian, Hispanic, or mixed-race descent. He was 5'03" to 5'09" tall and had been deceased between one and 20 years. His clothing tags were size large and extra large. This case is through Snohomish County Medical Examiner's Office.

This individual had nearly full dentals except for postmortem tooth loss of his right mandibular canine. He appeared to have an overbite. The skull had to be partially rebuilt, but most features seemed even and somewhat symmetrical. The biggest challenge on this case was to make his ancestry ambiguous and be able to be interpreted in different ways.

# 5

# CHAPTER 5

# The Eye and Brow

*The eyeball is centered in the orbital cavity. The eyelid attaches laterally to the Whitnall's or Malar Tubercle, and medially along the lacrimal fossa. The eyebrow follows the Supraorbital rim. The eye is 25 mm in size, and the iris is 11 to 13 mm.*

There are differences between the eyes in both sexes and all ancestries, and aging also must be taken into consideration when drawing the eyes. The four muscles shown in Figure 5.1 all contribute to the expressions of the eye, and therefore affect the eye and brow when aging. The terms shown on the left eye in Figure 5.2 are used in various studies, and can be useful in discussing the eye.

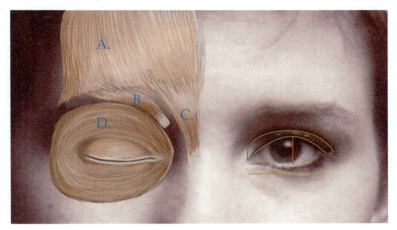

A  Frontalis
B  Corrugator supercilii
C  Procerus
D  Orbicularis oculi

Palpebral fissure length   Palpebral fissure height
Pretarsal

**Figure 5.1** The muscles that affect the eye and brow area pictured on the left, and terms used when discussing parts of the eye are pictured on the right.

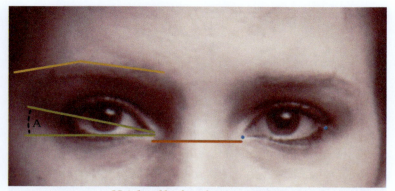

Height of highest brow point HBP
Intercanthal plane (angle A)
Distance between medial canthi DMC
Medial canthus and lateral canthus

**Figure 5.2** Additional reference terms for the eye and brow.

# The eyeball

Studies recently have noted that the eye is not centered in the orbital cavity.[1][2][3] Instead, the eyeball should be placed higher and wider than initially thought. Stephan places the eyeball 1.4mm above and 2.4mm lateral from the center of the orbital cavity. The lateral measurement makes a large difference as you move the eyeball wider on each eye, thus doubling the 2.4mm change from the center line of the face when you see both eyes. The eyes would then be 4.8mm further apart than initially thought. Additionally, Stephan measured the eyeball from all four sides of the orbit and gives the result as:

4mm from the supraorbital rim
6.8mm from the floor of the orbital cavity
4.5mm from the lateral wall
6.5mm from the medial wall

Pierre Guyomarc'h illustrates the correct placement in this image:

# THE EYE AND BROW

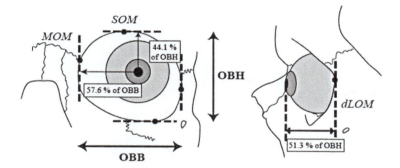

FIG. 2—*Proportional placement of the eyeball using the medial (MOM), superior (SOM), and deepest point of the lateral (dLOM) orbital margins with the percentages of the orbital height (OBH) and breadth (OBB).*

**Figure 5.3** Pierre Guyomarc'h uses this illustration to show proper placement of the eyeball in the orbital cavity. Here he marks the superior (sk), medial (mf), lateral (ec), and inferior (or) orbital margins. dLOM refers to the deepest point of the lateral margin. OBH is the orbital height, OBB is the orbital breadth.

Instead of millimeters off center, Guyomarc'h uses the percentage of the orbital cavity as a whole. He shows the center of the eyeball as 44.1% lower than the superior edge of the orbital cavity and 57.6% from the medial edge.

Illustrated on a skull, the differences are shown below.

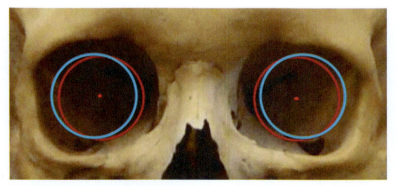

**Figure 5.4** The center of the orbital cavities is indicated by a red dot, and the centered eyeball is a red circle. The blue circles are raised about 1.5mm and moved laterally 2.5mm each.

I tested out this information on a few skulls with life photos. The results are below.

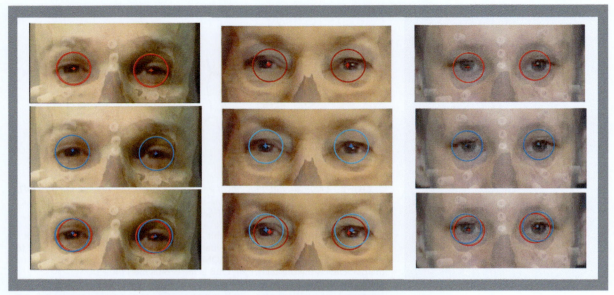

**Figure 5.5** Three subjects showing skulls with life photos overlaid. The red dot in the top image is the center of the orbital cavity, and the red circle is the corresponding eyeball placement. As seen, the red dot and circle do not match up with the iris in any image. The second image shows the blue dot with the adjusted placement of the eyeball and the corresponding blue circle for eyeball placement. This blue dot and blue circle are centered side to side in each image more closely than the red dot images. The bottom image for each shows a comparison overlay of both placements. It can be seen in each case that the eyeball falls more naturally into the blue circle location.

Per Whitnall, the inner canthus (corner) of the eye is located 2mm lateral to the middle of the lacrimal crest and the outer canthus is 3 to 4mm medial to the malar tubercle. There is a lateral and posterior lacrimal crest in the orbital cavity, and the lacrimal fossa forms the channel between the two.

THE EYE AND BROW  79

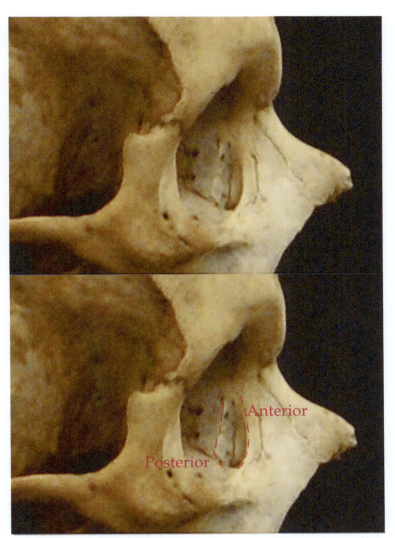

**Figure 5.6** The anterior and posterior lacrimal crests (marked in lower image). The lacrimal fossa is the channel between the two. Tears flow through the lacrimal fossa. The center of the lacrimal crest would be a vertical line down the middle of this channel.

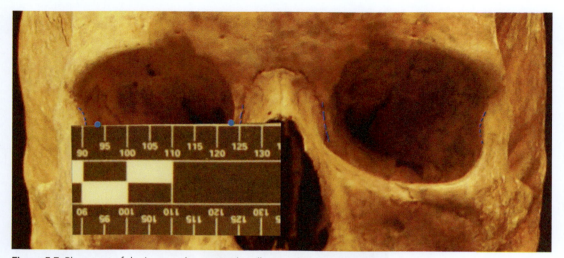

**Figure 5.7** Placement of the inner and outer canthus illustrated on the right side of the skull, per Whitnall. The Whitnall or Malar tubercle is marked on the lateral edges of the orbital cavity, and the middle of the lacrimal crest is marked on the medial edges of the orbital cavity on both sides of the skull for clarity. In this case, the placement of the inner canthus coincides with the posterior lacrimal crest. That is not the case in all skulls. Note that the medial eyelid attachment will be lower horizontally than the lateral attachment to promote tear drainage.

In regards to eyeball protrusion, previous teachings said that the eye is approximately flush with the bony rim in profile. If the artist drew a tangent line vertically from the vicinity of the base of tissue depth marker 12 above the center of the orbital cavity to the base of tissue depth marker 13 below the center of the orbital cavity, the eyeball would touch that line in profile. Dr. Caroline Wilkinson did a study in 2003[4] using 39 White adult males and females between 60 and 90 years of age. Her study showed the eyeball protruding past that tangent line in every case. Measurements showed the tangent line touching the iris, not the cornea, and the cornea protruding another 3.8mm beyond that line. Additionally, if the artist measures the orbital depth, the protrusion can be calculated with the formula:

Eyeball protrusion = 18.3 − (0.4 × orbit depth)

Consideration must be made that considers the thickness and overhang of the supraorbital rim and the inclination of the tangent line.

# THE EYE AND BROW

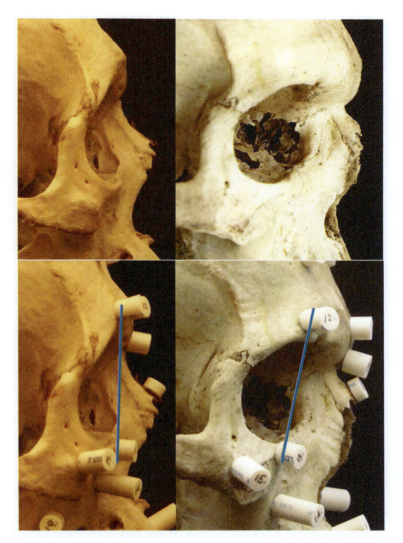

**Figure 5.8** A comparison between two different orbital cavities. The vertical tangent from superior to inferior orbital margin at the base of tissue depth markers 12 to 13 is shown. The subject on the left has a more vertically-inclined tangent illustrating average eye depth. The subject on the right is canted forward more due to the stronger brow ridge, indicating a deeper-set eye. Note that according to Wilkinson, the iris would touch this line but the cornea would extend past it 3.8mm.

When it comes to the shape of the eyelid and eyebrow, most sources refer to Fedosyutkin and Nainys.[5] Their research was published in 1993, but their information still appears to be the generally accepted method for this region of the face.

# The eyelid

Fedosyutkin and Nainys say the shape of the eyelid reflects the structure of the supraorbital rim. An average supraorbital rim will have an overhang in the middle section, which is reflected in the fold of the eyelid.

**Figure 5.9** An average supraorbital rim with overhang in middle section. Skull photos and life photo of same individual. Notice the vertical tangent of the orbital cavity and lack of brow ridge, resulting in an average depth eye with an even eyelid the full width of the eye.

When referring to a center overhang, it appears to mean the medial part of the supraorbital rim rolls back softly from the nasal bone. The center portion of the supraorbital rim takes a turn or fold. The outer portion continues that fold without change.

**Figure 5.10** Drawing the average eye and brow.

They advise if the outer rim is thickened and "slanted to the back of the upper side of the orbit," the eyelid fold will be more lateral. In this case, the lateral portion of the supraorbital rim shows a wider and more substantial edge.

If the orbital cavity is "high" with a low or medium-height nasal bridge and a long lacrimal fossa, the eyelid fold will be more medially placed. You usually will not see this in an eye of a person with Asian ancestry because of the structure of the epicanthic fold. The depth of the eyelid medially does not lend itself to the shape of an eye with an epicanthic fold.

THE EYE AND BROW  **83**

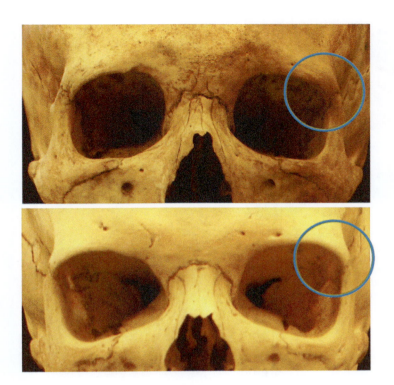

**Figure 5.11** This is the area to examine when considering a thickened lateral edge in the top image to the supraorbital cavity vs an average edge in the bottom image.

**Figure 5.12** A lateral eyelid fold. A good way to recall this is to picture the thickened lateral rim pushing down on the lateral portion of the eyelid, making the eyelid appear thinner top to bottom than it is medially. As the person ages, that portion of the eyelid will also have an overhang of flesh, causing the fold on the lateral part of the lid. Notice that the eyes still appear more open and expanded here, not as closed down and protected as they would be with a heavy brow ridge.

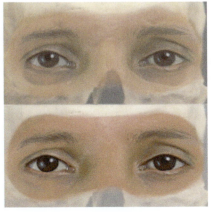

**Figure 5.13** Drawing the lateral eye fold. Top view allows skull to show through.

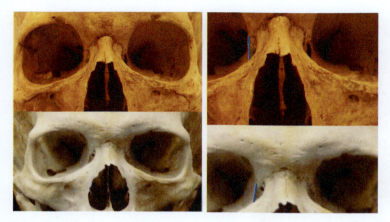

**Figure 5.14** Top image orbital cavities are high. On the lower image, the cavities look low. Note that the top cavities appear more open while the lower cavities look more closed vertically and protected. The lacrimal fossa, as a result, is longer in the top image. This is measured here as the base of the orbital opening at the lacrimal fossa to the frontonasal suture. The lower image eyes would be more shaded beneath the overhang of the brow ridge, and not as wide and round as the upper eyes.

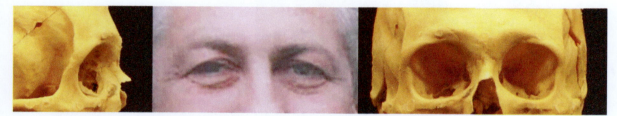

**Figure 5.15** Medial eyelid fold.

An open round orbit with a low nasal root indicates an epicathic fold. "Low nasal root" refers to the space between the eyes, also called the bridge of the nose. Commonly, those with Asian ancestry have a bridge that does not rise as high as those with European ancestry.

**Figure 5.16** Drawing the medial eye fold. This fold extends further medially than the lateral fold and often gives the eye a more protected appearance. Eyebrows tend to be lower. This eye looks more closed down and shielded by the brow ridge.

THE EYE AND BROW   85

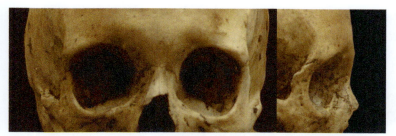

**Figure 5.17** Orbital structure indicating epicanthic fold. Observe the slight angle of the profile of the nose. The space between the orbital cavities does not rise as high, the bridge of the nose is low.

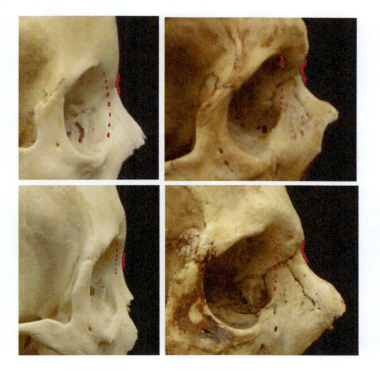

**Figure 5.18** Left side images show a low nasal root. Right side images show average to high nasal root. Look for the space between the medial portion of the orbital cavity and the front edge of the bridge of the nose, as marked in red on these images.

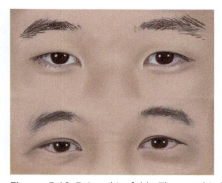

**Figure 5.19** Epicanthic fold. These orbital cavities would be open and round with a low nasal root between them.

## The eyebrow

In regards to eyebrows, Balueva and Lebedinskaya[6] and Fedosyutkin and Nainys have illustrated four different eyebrow shapes dependent on the supraorbital margin, brow ridge, and nasal root.

A strong brow ridge and supraorbital margin results in a low and straight eyebrow. A strong brow ridge is most commonly a male trait.

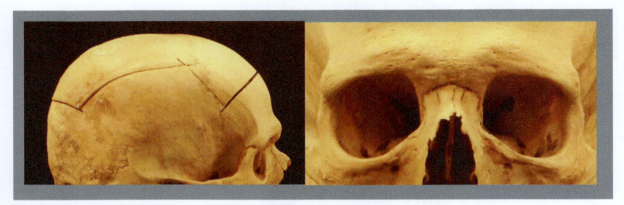

**Figure 5.20** Strong brow ridge and supraorbital margin on the skull.

Fedosyutkin and Nainys say a weak brow ridge and low nasal root results in an S-shaped eyebrow. Wilkinson describes this more clearly as the medial third of the eyebrow being located beneath the supraorbital rim, while the lateral two-thirds of the eyebrow slopes up to the supraorbital margin and then traces the contour. A weaker brow ridge is often a more feminine trait. The low nasal root is more commonly found in people of Asian or African-derived ancestry.

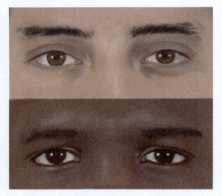

**Figure 5.21** Strong brow and supraorbital margin eyebrow form and how it appears on the face. The eye is in shadow from the brow ridge and brows are usually close to the eye and straight.

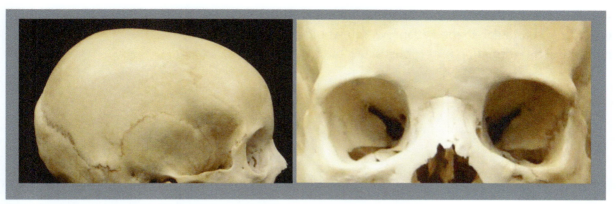

**Figure 5.22** Weak brow ridge and low nasal root on the skull.

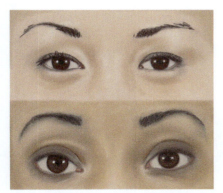

A weak brow ridge and high nasal root results in an arched or rounded eyebrow. The higher nasal root is more commonly found in European-derived ancestry.

**Figure 5.23** Weak brow ridge and low nasal root eyebrow form and how it appears on the face.

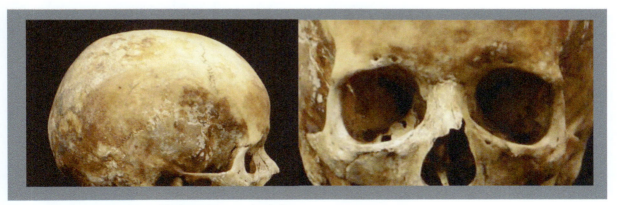

**Figure 5.24** Weak brow ridge and high nasal root on the skull.

A strong brow ridge with thickened lateral supraorbital rim results in a triangular-shaped eyebrow. You would more commonly find this formation on a robust skull.

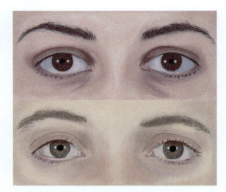

**Figure 5.25** Weak brow ridge and high nasal root eyebrow form as it appears on the face. This is quite similar to the weak brow ridge and low nasal root, but medially starts higher on the supraorbital rim.

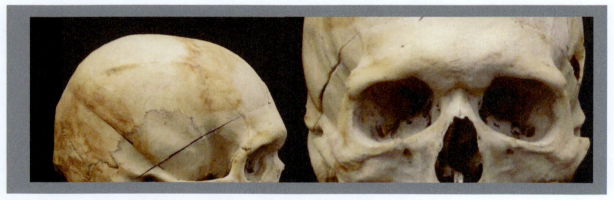

**Figure 5.26** Strong brow ridge and thickened lateral supraorbital rim on the skull.

# The brow ridge

If an artist does not get many cases each year, they may be unsure what qualifies as a thickened lateral supraorbital rim and what is average. I illustrate thickened and average lateral supraorbital rims below. When drawing this type of skull, it indicates a heavy brow ridge. Often, the eye area is shaded by the brow ridge. Be aware the complete skull should be robust as well and consider this with the rest of the features.

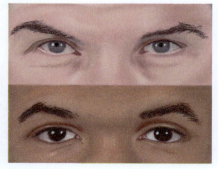

**Figure 5.27** Strong brow ridge and thickened lateral supraorbital rim eyebrow form on the face.

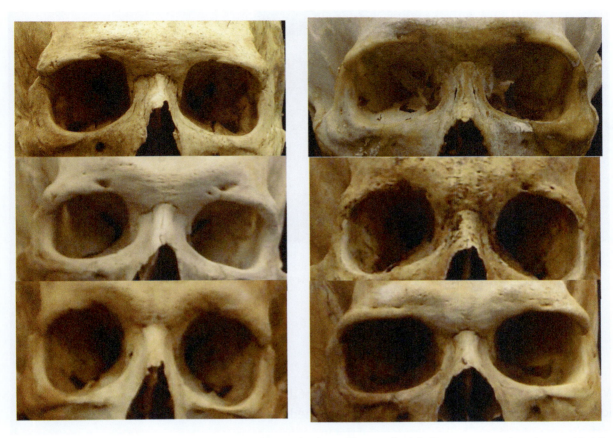

**Figure 5.28** The skulls on the left show thickened lateral supraorbital rims. Those on the right illustrate average lateral supraorbital rims. All the skulls show an average to heavy brow ridge.

For the most part, the strong brow ridge is considered a male trait but be careful to not make assumptions. In Figure 5.29, I illustrate a case where a female skull had deepset eyes that look like she had a brow ridge. Be sure to draw what the skull is showing you, not what you believe should be there.

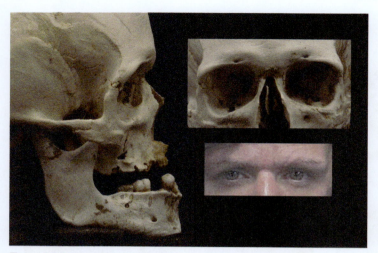

**Figure 5.29** This skull is female, but her eyes are deepset, forming a bit of a brow ridge shading her orbital cavities. Notice the forehead above the glabella is vertical like a typical female skull, but the mandible is shaped in a more masculine manner. This female was average in size.

# The eye opening

When drawing the opening of the eye, the height of the upper lid where it touches the eye is generally greater medially, not in the center of the lid. The lowest point of the lower lid where it touches the eye is more lateral, also not in the center of the lid. The lateral canthus hugs the eyeball while the medial canthus flares away from the eyeball to attach to the lacrimal fossa. This means the lateral canthal angle is larger than the medial canthal angle, as laterally the eyelid is curving in around the ball and medially it is pulling straight away from the ball to attach further forward on the facial plane. The upper eyelid overlaps the lower at the lateral canthus. The eyelids (in most cases) touch the iris superiorly and inferiorly.

**Figure 5.30** Shows where to place the eyeball in the skull. The circle represents the eyeball in the orbital cavity. The outline shows the shape of the opening of the eye, and where the tarsal plates of the eyelids attach to the skull with the canthal tendons. Medially, the tendons attach to both the front and back of the lacrimal fossa. The overhead view shows the facial plane, and how the medial attachment is much further forward than the lateral attachment.

## Aging the eye and brow

Knize[7] has observed through anatomical study of twenty fresh cadaver specimens that the lateral eyebrow almost always descends earlier than the medial in aging populations. He finds the soft tissue relatively unsupported laterally in the eye and forehead region. He advises the frontalis muscle has a consistent relationship with the temporal fusion line, ending laterally along or just lateral to that line. This results in the frontalis not being as wide as the eyebrow, leaving the lateral part of the brow unsupported by the frontalis and more likely to droop before the medial part. (See Figure 5.31).

This results in excess skin in the lateral eyelid area as the brow descends into the orbital space. The drooping is called ptosis. Yun et al.[8] studied aging and the eyebrow using thirty-six female Korean subjects and came to a similar conclusion. They found that the younger subjects engaged the frontalis and the corrugator supercilii muscles significantly more than the older subjects when making facial expressions. The older subjects engaged the orbicularis oculi more than the younger subjects. Yun believes this shows that the frontalis and corrugator get age-related muscular weakness but that, because of constant blinking, the orbicularis oculi becomes stronger. If a person blinks 10 to 12 times a minute, it adds up to about 6000 activations for the orbicularis oculi per day. Activation of the

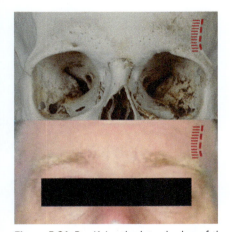

**Figure 5.31** Per Knize the lateral edge of the frontalis muscle is related to the temporal fusion line, indicated by vertical dashed line above. Medial to that line is what he calls a "zone of fixation," indicated by horizontal dashes. Laterally to that zone is the temporalis fascia and muscle, which run perpendicular to the frontalis. Note how much eyebrow is lateral to the zone of fixation, which means the frontalis muscle does not affect that portion of the brow.

frontalis and corrugator supercilii per day would be much less frequent. This could explain why the orbicularis oculi remains strong as we age and the frontalis and corrugator wither. He believes the strength of the orbicularis oculi might create a continuous strong downward force that contributes to sagging eyebrows as we age. This study also referenced the frontalis muscle having less of an influence on the lateral part of the brow, leading to the brow and eyelid ptosis.

Asaad et al.[9] reviewed nineteen articles regarding eyebrow height changes and aging, consisting of 3634 patients of various ancestries. They found the articles reported the eyebrows showed significant increase with aging at the medial canthus and the mid-pupil. There is speculation that older people raise their brows medially in order to lift the skin that is sagging over their eyes to see better, resulting in a brow that is higher medially than when the subjects were younger. Asaad concluded the eyebrow height remained stable at the lateral canthus but decreased at the lateral eyebrow end.

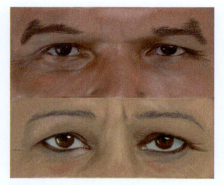

**Figure 5.32** Aging lateral brow is unsupported by frontalis muscle, resulting in lateral eyelid ptosis.

## Ancestry and gender differences

There are studies that have looked at differences in brows and eyelids in different ancestries and genders. Price et al.[10] researched eyelid and eyebrow dimensions in 164 African American and Caucasian patients divided into gender and age groups: 20 to 39, 40 to 59, 60 to 79.

## Regarding eyelids

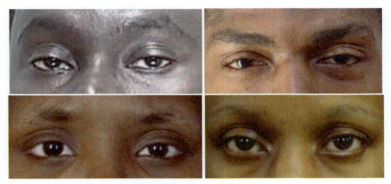

Double lid crease

**Figure 5.33** Double eyelid crease, more commonly found in African-derived populations.

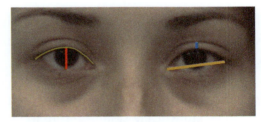

Palpebral fissure height
Pretarsal skin height
Pretarsal skin crease
Fissure slant

**Figure 5.34** Additional eye terms used in this study.

37% of African Americans had at least one lid with a double lid crease, compared with 15% of Whites.

Black females had greater fissure slants than Black males, significant in youngest and middle ages.

Black males had significantly greater palpebral fissure width and higher pretarsal skin height and crease height than White males in the oldest group (60-79).

Young White females had significantly greater palpebral fissure height and inclination (intercanthal plane) than White males. White females had a greater pretarsal skin height and crease height than White males, statistically significant in the youngest group.

White females had significantly greater palpebral fissure width than White males in the oldest group.

Very few differences were found for palpebral fissure measurements between races. Prior studies found the palpebral fissure length (width) shortened by approx. 10% after age 45, and a gradual decrease in width with age.

Regarding eyebrows

Black male mean eyebrow height was greater compared with White male. Black males had significantly higher eyebrow height in the oldest group compared with Black males in the middle age group.

Brow apex angle is greater in women than in men in almost all groups but only statistically significant in the middle age group of African Americans.

Black females had greater mean eyebrow height than White females in all ages, but only statistically significant in 40-59 ages. They also showed significantly greater eyebrow height than Black males in the youngest and middle age groups.

White females had significantly greater eyebrow height than White males.

Odunze et al.[11] studied the lateral canthal complex and came to some of the same conclusions as Price. They studied 296 cases of African American and Caucasian patients and report statistically significant intrarace differences in the lateral canthal angle. They found the median lateral canthal angle for African Americans 45 years of age or younger to be 3.00 degrees, decreasing to 1.15 degrees for patients older than 45. In Caucasian patients, the younger group showed 2.3 degrees, decreasing to 1.30 degrees for the older group.

Kraus et al.[12] also studied age and sex-dependent changes in eyebrow height and shape in 244 Caucasian patients divided into groups by age, under 34 and over 55.

Data showed a difference between brow shapes of young females and males, especially relating to the HBP (height of highest brow point), which is located medially in young females. The brow shape of females assimilates toward a male shape with aging. In most cases, the eyebrow HBP is at the lateral limbus, or directly above the lateral edge of the iris.

The eyebrow moves upward, the DMC (distance between medial canthi) widens, and the lid axis drops laterally in both sexes with aging. With aging, the HBP was located higher and more laterally in both genders.

There is statistically significant flattening of the intercanthal plane in aging in both genders.

While they found barely any difference in the height of the upper brow border comparing both genders in the same age group, the position and height of the HBP differs particularly between young females and males. The HBP in young males is located higher and more laterally than that in young females. This suggests the brow is more angled in young males, whereas it is rounder in young females. It can be concluded that the contour of the upper brow border and the height, as well as the position of the HBP, becomes more similar in both genders as they grow older. The upper brow line moves upward with increasing age, especially in females. This may be due to more widespread frontalis hyperactivity. In this study, the intercanthal plane flattens with aging.

Note that this study did not differentiate between medial and lateral parts of the eyebrow. Other studies have shown the medial part of the brow moving upward, but the lateral part moving downward. This is the only study that I have found that shows the brows rising with aging.

Van den Bosch et al.[13] advise that aging makes an impact on the horizontal eyelid fissure. They found it lengthens by more than 10% between 12 and 25 years of age (probably reflecting growth of the facial structures). After the age of 45, they found the fissure decreased by the same amount. They surmised this was because of increasing laxity of medial and lateral canthal structures as we age. They also found aging causes a downward shift in the lower eyelid, primarily in men.

I have not found a lot of articles about Asian eyes, but I did locate one study by Park et al.[14] While they did not discuss eyebrows, they did analyze the palpebral fissure length, height, and angle in 234 Asian males and 264 Asian females. They found the palpebral fissure length was slightly more in males while the height was slightly more in females. They measured the average slant of the palpebral fissure to be 7.9 ± 2.4 degrees in males and 8.8 ± 2.3 degrees in females. The average interpupillary distance was slightly higher in males.

## Four eyebrow shapes in summary

To summarize the four eyebrow shapes, here they are in a group together.

**Figure 5.35** Examples of Asian eyes. Females on left, males on right.

THE EYE AND BROW   97

**Figure 5.36** Strong brow and supraorbital margin = low and straight brow.

**Figure 5.37** Strong brow and thick supraorbital rim = triangular brow.

**Figure 5.38** Weak brow and high nasal root = curved brow.

**Figure 5.39** Weak brow and low nasal root = s shaped brow.

# Notes

1 Stephan, Carl, Davidson, Paavi. (2008). The Placement of the Human Eyeball and Canthi in Craniofacial Identification. *Journal of Forensic Sciences, 53*(3) 612–619.https://onlinelibrary.wiley.com/doi/abs/10.1111/j.1556-4029.2008.00718.x

2 Stephan, Carl, et al. (2009). Further Evidence on the Anatomical Placement of the Human Eyeball for Facial Approximation and Craniofacial Superimposition. *Journal of Forensic Sciences, 54*(2), 267–269.https://onlinelibrary.wiley.com/doi/full/10.1111/j.1556-4029.2008.00982x

3 Guyomarc'h, Pierre et al. (2012) Anatomical Placement of the Human Eyeball in the Orbit – Validation Using CT Scans of Living Adults and Prediction for Facial Approximation. L'Universite' Bordeaux 1, Anthropologie Biologique dissertation. https://theses.fr/2011BOR14354#

4 Wilkinson, Caroline M. & Mautner, Sophie A. (2003) Measurement of Eyeball Protrusion and Its Application in Facial Reconstruction. *Journal of Forensic Sciences, 48*(1) 12–16. www.astm.org/digital_library/journals/forensic/pages/jfs2002053.htm

5 Fedosyutkin, Boris A. & Nainys, Jonas V. (1993). The Relationship of Skull Morphology to Facial Features. In Iscan, Mehmet Yasar & Helmer, Richard P. Eds. *Forensic Analysis of the Skull* (199–213) Wiley-Liss.

6 Balueva, T. S., & Lebedinskaya, G. V. (1991). Anthropological reconstruction. *Moscow: Russian Academy of Sciences.*

7 Knize, D. M. (1996) An Anatomically Based Study of the Mechanism of Eyebrow Ptosis. *Plastic and Reconstructive Surgery,* 1321–1333. https://journals.lww.com/plasreconsurg/abstract/1996/06000/an_anatomically_based_study_of_the_mechanism_of.1.aspx

8   Yun, Sangho, et al. (2014) Changes of Eyebrow Muscle Activity with Aging: Functional Analysis Revealed by Electromyography. *Plastic and Reconstructive Surgery*, 455e-463e. https://researchgate.net/publication/259498582_changes_of_eyebrow_muscle_activity_with_aging

9   Asaad, Malke, et al. (2019) Eyebrow Height Changes with Aging: A Systematic Review and Meta-analysis. *Plastic and Reconstructive Surgery Global Open*, 1–10. https://pubmed.ncbi.nlm.nih.gov/pmc/articles/pmc6908395/

10  Price, Kristina M, et al. (2009) Eyebrow and Eyelid Dimensions: An Anthropometric Analysis of African Americans and Caucasians. *Plastic and Reconstructive Surgery*, 615–623. https://pubmed.ncbi.nlm.nih.gov/19644282/

11  Odunze, Millicent, et al. (2008) Periorbital Aging and Ethnic Considerations: A Focus on the Lateral Canthal Complex. *Plastic and Reconstructive Surgery*, *121*(3), 1002–1008. https://journals.lww.com/plasreconsurg/abstract/2008/03000/periorbital_aging_and_ethnic_considerations_a.37.aspx

12  Kraus, Daniel et al. (2019) A morphometric study of age- and sex-dependent changes in eyebrow height and shape. *Journal of Plastic, Reconstructive & Aesthetic Surgery*. *72*(6) 1012–1019. www.sciencedirect.com/science/article/abs/pii/s1748681519300324

13  van den Bosch, Willem, et al. (1999) Topographic anatomy of the eyelids, and the effects of sex and age. *British Journal of Ophthalmology*, *83*, 347–352. https://bjo.bmj.com/content/83/3/347.

14  Park, Dae Hwan, et al. (2008) Anthropometry of Asian Eyelids by Age. *Plastic and Reconstructive Surgery*, *121*(4), 1405–1413. https://journals.lww.com/plasreconsurg/abstract/2008/04000/anthropometry_of)asian_eyelids_by_age.44.aspx

# 6

# CHAPTER 6

# The Nose

*Measure the length of the nasal spine from tip to vomer. Multiply that number by 3 to get the total length of the nose. On the profile photo of the skull, estimate the angle of the nose from the direction that the nasal spine in pointing. Beginning at the end of tissue depth marker #5, add the total length that you just established at the predetermined angle. On the anterior photo of the skull, the nostrils are each 5mm wider than the nasal opening for a Caucasian-derived skull and 8mm wider on each side for an African-derived skull. The nostrils attach 4 or 5 mm below the nasal opening. A pointed nasal spine equates to a pointed nose while a nasal spine with a wide blunt tip equates to a nose with a wide blunt tip.*

For our purposes, we do not have many muscles to be aware of around the nose. The nasalis contracts to dilate the nostrils, depress the nostril wings, and wrinkle the nose. The levator labii superioris alaeque nasi pulls the upper lip and wing of the nose. The nasal cavity is also referred to as the piriform aperture.

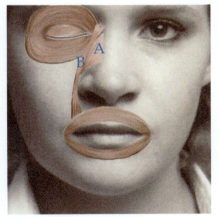

A nasalis
B levator labii superioris alaeque nasi

**Figure 6.1** Muscles associated with the nose. Photo of a face with overlaid illustration of muscles associated with the nose: the nasalis and the levator labii superioris alaeque nasi.

The nose has always been a challenging feature to interpret. The angle of the nose is difficult to estimate from the skull. In Krogman's[1] method (above in italic), a great deal depends on the direction of the nasal spine. It has not been clearly explained how to assess the angle of the spine correctly.

DOI: 10.4324/9781003285588-6

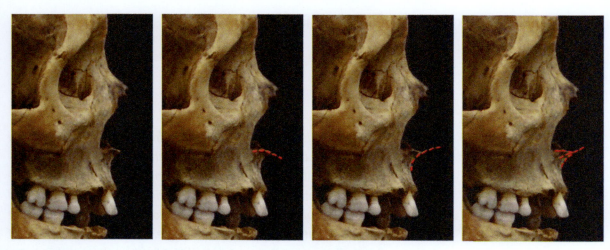

**Figure 6.2** The profile view of the nasal spine. It is incorrect to extend either the horizontal or the vertical part of the spine to estimate the direction of the nose. It is also incorrect to assess a halfway point between these two edges.

Previous texts advise to use the direction that the spine is pointing, which is not the same as dividing in half to find the exact center of the horizontal and vertical directions. It seems a bit unclear and could be interpreted in slightly dissimilar ways by each artist. It also does not work if the nasal spine is broken or missing, as happens in many cases. Leaving this important feature up to intuition does not seem the best course of action.

When beginning a reconstruction, most artists start out with photos of the profile and the anterior of the skull side by side. I do as well. I do not however take the profile drawing to a full finished stage, as I believe it is unnecessary. The medical examiner does not release a profile along with the anterior drawing in my experience. I use the profile only in order to establish the size and shape of the nose and to learn information about the ears and outline of the facial profile. I refer to it as I progress in the anterior drawing, but I do not take it to a completed state or send it with the anterior drawing to the detective at the end of the job.

In the past several years, I have been using Chris Rynn's[2] method instead of Krogman's. This method can appear daunting at first, but I will illustrate how to do it step by step. This approach can be done using profile photos with or without tissue depth markers. I am illustrating it without the markers so the placement on the skull is clearer. Once the nose shape is determined, it can be transferred into the image that has tissue depth markers.

## Chris Rynn's method

Instead of keeping the skull in the Frankfort Horizontal Plane, Rynn starts by rotating the skull into the Nasion Prosthion Plane (NPP), where the nasion and prosthion are lined up vertically. The nasion is the bridge of the nose, where tissue depth marker 3 is placed. The prosthion is the point on the alveolar arch midway between the median maxillary incisor teeth, where tissue depth marker 6 is placed.

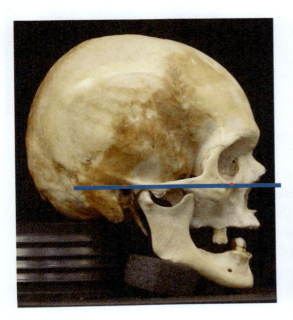
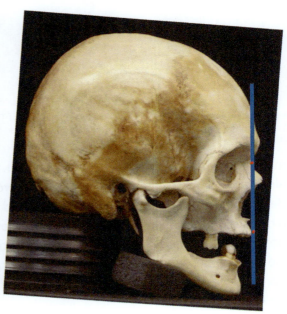

**Figure 6.3** Left image shows skull in Frankfort Horizontal Plane: the top of the external auditory meatus is on a horizontal plane with the inferior border of the orbital cavity. Right image shows skull in Nasion Prosthion Plane: the nasion is on a vertical plane with the prosthion. As each skull is different, the amount of change rotating the skull off the angle of the FHP will vary with each case.

A series of four points is placed on the skull. Three of these points correspond to the locations where tissue depth markers are placed: TDM 3, TDM 4, and TDM 5. The other point is placed at the end of the nasal spine.

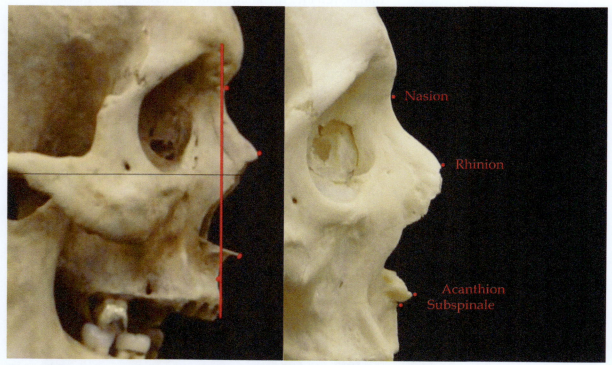

**Figure 6.4** Placing the four points. They are located at the base of TDM 3, TDM 4, TDM 5, and at the end point of the nasal spine. The names of those locations (from top to bottom) are nasion, rhinion, acanthion, and subspinale.

The measurements require a ruler from this point. If working digitally, copy and paste the ruler that is on the profile photo in order to have a ruler that can be moved around the image and is the correct size. Make sure the ruler is on its own layer. If you are working in pencil, confirm the photo is printed out and sized so that the measurements on the ruler in the photo match those on your physical ruler.

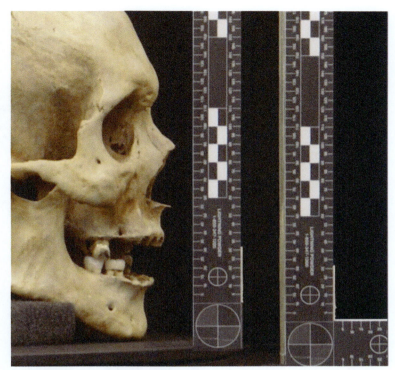

**Figure 6.5** Copy the ruler from the image to have a ruler that can be moved around the image.

Rynn measures a series of three lines between the four points. The first is the 'x' line. Move the ruler to measure from the base of TDM 3 to the end of the nasal spine and make a notation of the length of that line. This is the nasion to the acanthion.

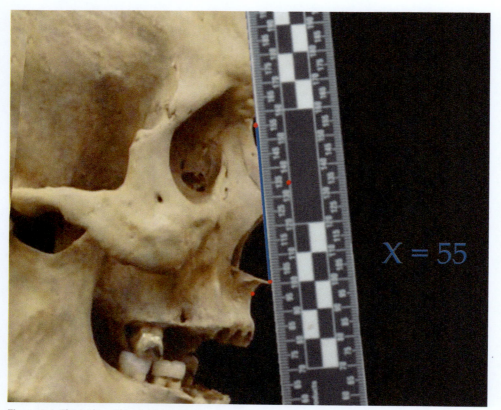

**Figure 6.6** The 'x' line. This skull shows 55mm for this length.

The 'y' line is next. It is measured from the base of TDM 4 to the base of TDM 5. This is the rhinion to the subspinale.

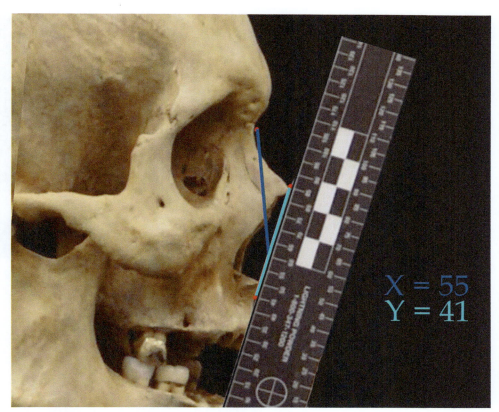

**Figure 6.7** The 'y' line on this skull measures 41mm.

The last line, 'z', is measured from the base of TDM 3 to the base of TDM 5. This is the nasion to the subspinale.

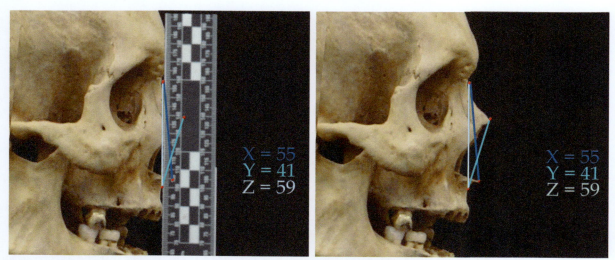

**Figure 6.8** The 'z' line on this skull measures 59mm. The second image shows all lines complete without the ruler.

Once all four points are plotted and measured, there are equations to determine the length of the lines that will become the shape of the nose.

**Table 6.1** Chris Rynn's calculations to measure the nose. Adapted from *Prediction of Nasal Morphology from the Skull*.

| Number | Equation | Ancestry |
| --- | --- | --- |
| 1 | $0.83y - 3.5$ | All |
| 2 | $0.9x - 2$ | All |
| 3 | $0.93y - 6$ | All |
| 4 | $0.74z + 3.5$ | All |
| 5 | $0.63z + 17$ | European Females |
|   | $0.78z + 9.5$ | European Males |
| 6 | $0.5y + 1.5$ | All Females |
|   | $0.4y + 5$ | All Males |

It can appear daunting if you do not like doing math, but these are simple if you have a calculator.

For line 1 on this skull, the equation to enter on the calculator is .83 x 41. (41 is the measurement of y on this skull) When you have a result for that first part, then subtract 3.5 to get the result. (0.83 multiplied by y, minus 3.5.)

For line 2 on this skull, enter .9 x 55 (55 being the measurement of x on this skull), and then subtract 2 for the result. Continue similarly for the rest of the equations. Note that number five equation is only for European ancestry skulls and is different for males than for females. The number six equation is for all ancestries, but also divided into males and females. Use the measurement for the correct sex.

For this European male skull, the measurement totals are:

1) 30.53
2) 47.5
3) 32.13
4) 47.16
5) 55.52
6) 21.4

At this point, the x, y, and z lines are no longer required on the image. The points are still required. The artist can make the digital layer with the lines invisible. It is best to keep that information until the calculations are finished just to be sure everything is done correctly. If drawing in graphite, the artist can set aside that sheet of tracing paper and work on a new sheet of tracing paper or the vellum paper that will become the final drawing.

The reason the skull is in the NPP instead of FHP becomes clear at this point. Line 1 needs to be a horizontal line extending out from the base of TDM 3 while the skull is in NPP. If you begin drawing these measurements with the skull in FHP, the nose will be at the wrong angle. This may appear a complicated process, but take it step by step. Concentrate on completing each line properly before moving on to the next.

Line 1 will be measured projecting out from the profile of the skull on a horizontal. It starts at the base of TDM 3 or the nasion. Line 1 is 30.53mm, as previously calculated.

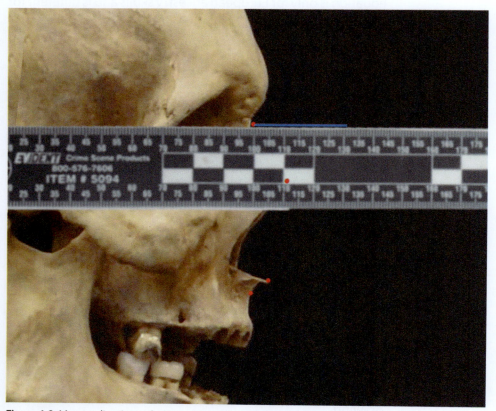

**Figure 6.9** Measure line 1 on a horizontal extending from the nasion. Line 1 on this skull is 30.53.

Line 2 is a vertical drop from the far end of line 1. We've calculated that to be 47.5mm.

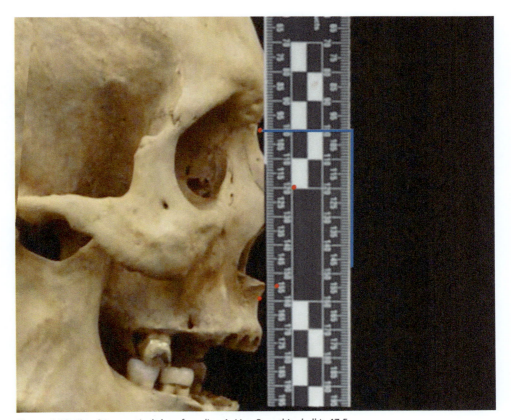

**Figure 6.10** Line 2 is a vertical drop from line 1. Line 2 on this skull is 47.5.

Line 3 is another horizontal line extending out from the base of TDM 5 or subspinale. We calculated line 3 to be 32.13mm.

**114** READING THE SKULL

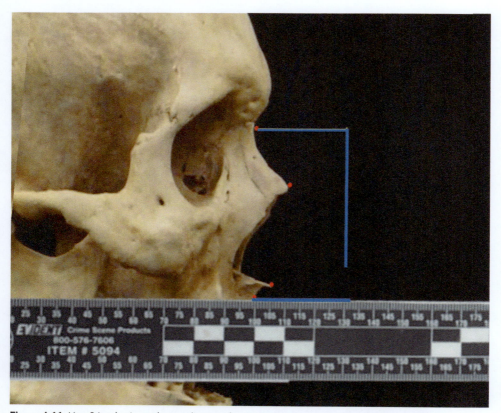

**Figure 6.11** Line 3 is a horizontal extending out from the subspinale. Line 3 on this skull is 32.13.

Line 4 shows the nasal length. To start for lines 4 and 5, the length of TDM 4 must be added to the profile to show the soft tissue measurement at that location. For a European male, that TDM length is 6.5mm.

THE NOSE 115

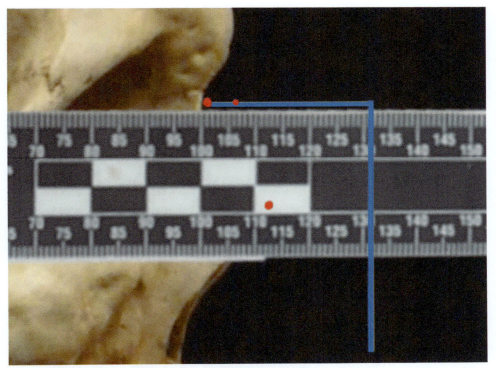

**Figure 6.12** The length of TDM 3 is added to the profile. For a European male, that measurement is 6.5mm. That point is plotted along line 1, 6.5mm away from the bone.

Line 4 begins at this new soft tissue point along line 1, and extends down on an angle to touch line 2. For this subject, this line will be 47.16mm. Find that length on the ruler and angle it until it starts at the new point and intersects with line 2.

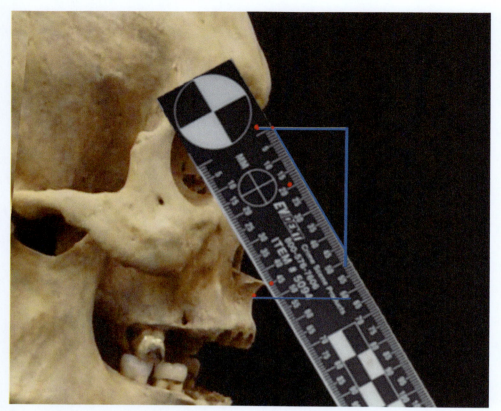

**Figure 6.13** Line 4 begins at the new soft tissue point along line 1, and angles down for the required measurement until it intersects with line 2. Find the 47mm mark on the ruler and rotate it from the upper point until it intersects with line 2.

A new soft tissue location point is also needed for line 5. The length of TDM 5 is plotted on the profile (for European males, that measurement is 10mm). The new point is placed on line 3, which extends horizontally from the base of TDM 5. Line 5 is then measured between the two soft tissue points. This line should equal the measurement determined for line 5, which is 55.52mm for this skull.

THE NOSE 117

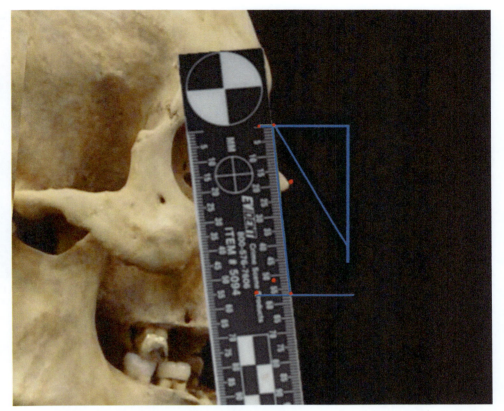

**Figure 6.14** Line 5 is placed from the two soft tissue points. If the equations are correct, this length should be the length determined in the equations for line 5. On this skull, this measurement is 55.52.

The final line is 6. This line angles up from the subspinale soft tissue point to intersect with line 2, which is the length and extension of the nose.

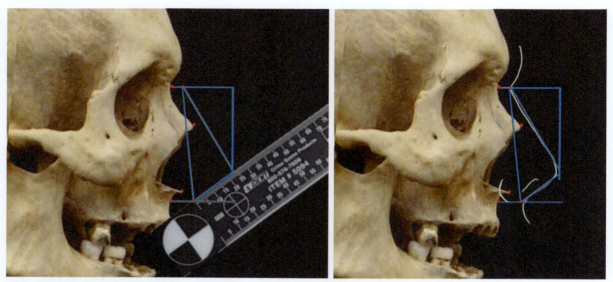

**Figure 6.15** Line 6 extends up on an angle from the subspinale soft tissue point of TDM 5 to intersect with the vertical line 2. For this individual, the measurement should be 21.4mm. The second image shows the nose drawn in with those measurements. The nose for this individual shows a lot of nostril. The point is high, not level or low.

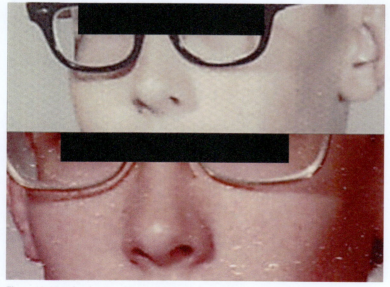

**Figure 6.16** Life photos of the individual whose skull was used in these examples.

There are two other methods that can be used to verify the profile measurements of the nose. The first again uses intuition to approximate the angle, but can be used if the artist is comfortable with their instincts. This would be the two-tangent method.

# The Two-Tangent method

The two-tangent method extends two lines that intersect at the point of the nose. The first line follows the main direction of the nasal bone in profile. It does not extend directly from the end of the bone, which frequently drops off in the last eighth of an inch or so, but is intuited by the artist as the direction the bone generally shows. (As in Krogman's method, this seems a little subjective. I use it for verification, not establishing the shape.) The second line duplicates the Krogman method, extending from the nasal spine in the direction that it also appears to point.

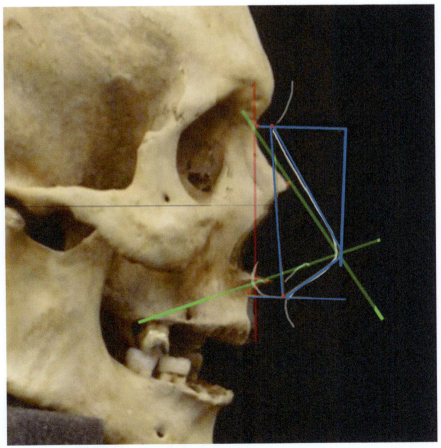

**Figure 6.17** The two-tangent method (in green) superimposed over the previously-ascertained shape of the nose.

## Prokopec and Ubelaker's method

The second method by Prokopec and Ubelaker[3] is similar to that shown by Lebedinskaya in 1974. It can be determined in four or five steps. I often use this one if I would like verification of Rynn's method.

With the skull returned to the FHP, a vertical line is drawn to intersect the nasion and the prosthion. This line would be completely vertical in the NPP, but must be rotated to touch those points in the FHP. Call this Line A.

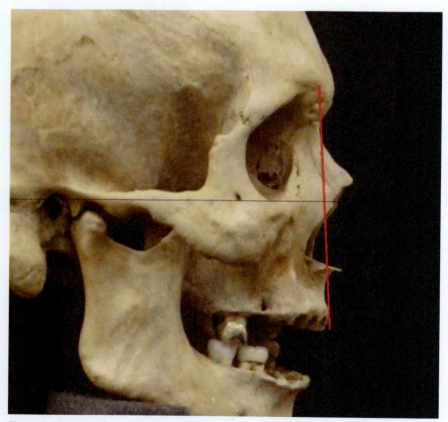

**Figure 6.18** Line A from nasion to prosthion. Skull is in the FHP. The line would be straight up and down in the NPP, but is slightly angled on this skull in the FHP. A different skull may have a steeper angle than this one.

THE NOSE    **121**

If the artist is working digitally, the second step is the duplicate the first line and move it so that it parallels this line but intersects the tip of the nasal bone. If working in pencil, this line is drawn by hand. Call this Line B.

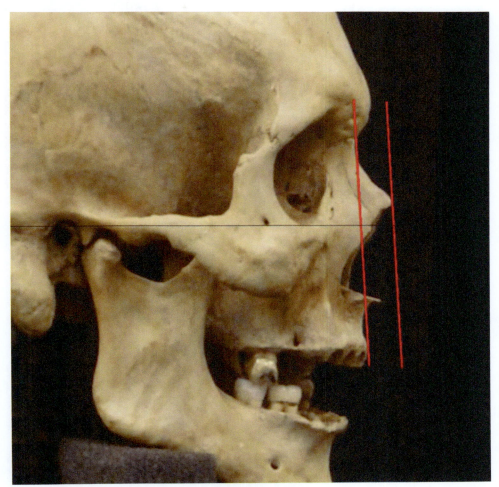

**Figure 6.19** Duplicate line A and move it so that it intersects with the tip of the nasal bone. This is Line B.

A series of parallel lines is drawn from the inferior tip of the nasal bone to the base of the piriform aperture. These lines need to be perpendicular to lines A and B, not flat horizontal lines, so they need to be rotated by the artist after drawing the lines straight on a horizontal in the digital software. The lines fill in the space between the nasal border and line B.

**122** READING THE SKULL

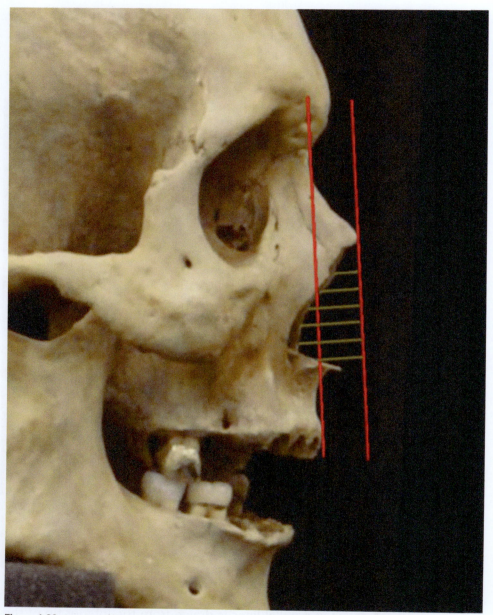

**Figure 6.20** A series of lines is drawn that follows the outline of the piriform aperture and extends to line B.

If drawing by hand, measure each of the parallel lines and extend them past Line B for the same distance, doubling the length of each line (making a mirror image of the original lines). If working digitally, duplicate that layer and flip it horizontally. The layer will need to be rotated again to keep the lines extending straight out from the original lines and perpendicular to lines A and B.

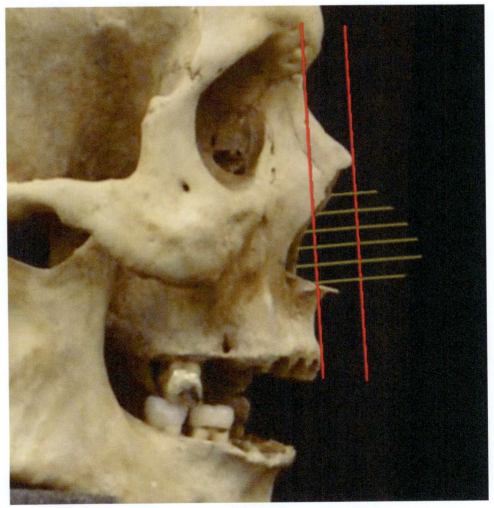

**Figure 6.21** Duplicate the parallel lines and flip to make a mirror image of them centered on Line B.

Connect the outer points of those lines to create the curve of the nose. Add about 2mm to account for thickness of skin and fat layer.

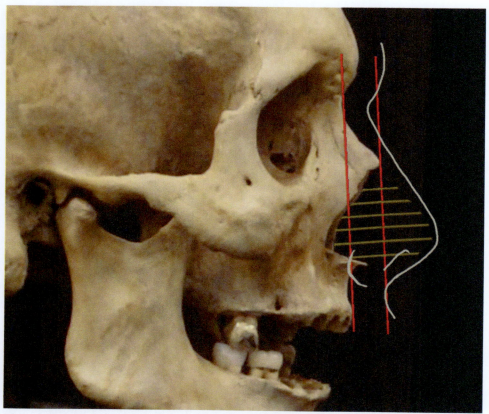

**Figure 6.22** Comparison of this method to the original nose measurements from Rynn's method.

## Davy-Jow's study

Additionally, more information can be determined for the tip of the nose from Stephanie Davy-Jow's study.[4] In studying 25 patients of various ages and both sexes, in 22 of them the curvature of the nose tip mimics the curvature of the superior portion of the piriform aperture. To find this, you must take a photo of the skull with the head rotated so that that bony outline is revealed.

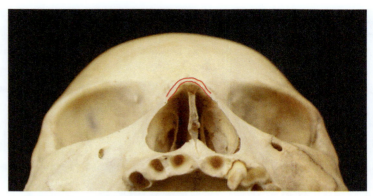

**Figure 6.23** Nose tip validation. Red lines show the superior border of the piriform aperture and the projected nose tip that echoes the shape of the border line.

An additional benefit to this method is that it also shows you if the nasal opening is leaning to one side or the other, impinging on the orbital cavity. It may also show you if the nostrils are uneven at both the sides and the base of the nasal opening. On this nose, her right nostril appears rounder and higher than the left. This should be confirmed by viewing the nose in the anterior perspective.

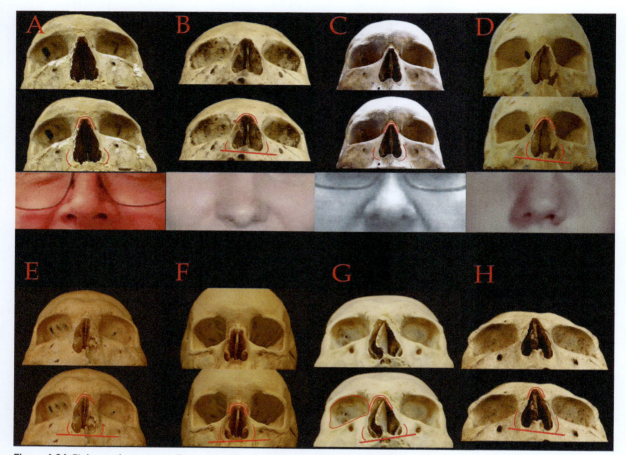

**Figure 6.24** Eight nasal openings, all in various shapes. The top images show a row of the skulls with no markings so they can be examined. The second row of skull photos are the same skulls with markings showing the nose tip shape along with other anomalies specific to that skull. Photos A through D show the identified person's nose below the second row of skull photos. There are no life photos for photos E through H.

In Figure 6.24, I show eight different skulls photographed in this rotation. Some are rotated more than others, as I have learned this over time and rotated at different angles to test the theory.

Skull A is a fairly even opening, but tips a little toward the right eye at the top of the nasal opening. (Unfortunately, the only photos that I have of the victim that are not unfocused show the face turned slightly in each and this tipping is not clearly evident.) Observe the angle of the nasal opening on either side, which impacts the lean to the nose in life and the shape of the midface as it flows from the nose. The nose tip looks squared off.

Skull B shows the right nostril higher than the left, which corresponds to the life photo. The top of the nasal opening looks wider than others. It appears the bridge of this nose is lower in the anterior photo, resulting in a wide and low nose. This individual's DNA showed her to be mixed race, which could account for the low nasal root or bridge more commonly associated with the African American part of her ancestry.

Skull C shows the right nostril subtly fuller—higher and wider—than the left. That is shown in the life photo of the victim. The nasal aperture is thinner and pointier, and the corresponding nasal bridge is high and defined. Compare this to the nose in Skull B.

Skull D shows the right nostril slightly higher than the left. Additionally, the shape of the nasal opening tips to the left at the bridge and is quite wide through the horizontal midpoint, making the nose more compact and tighter through the nostrils. As the mid-nose is wider, the nostrils do not look as wide in comparison.

Skull E shows the right nostril slight lower than the left and a rounded nasal tip.

Skull F shows a squared nasal tip and the right nostril lower than the left.

Skull G shows the right nostril lower than the left. Based on the inferior nasal concha, the right nostril is significantly taller and longer than the left. Also, the nose tips towards the right orbital cavity. The interior bones of the nose point to the right, which results in a nose that follows that shape. If doing a reconstruction on this skull, pay attention to the harmony of all the features together on the face.

Skull H shows a slender nose tip and the right nostril quite a bit higher and rounder than the left.

## Nostrils

When drawing nostrils, not just the width is ancestry-derived. The shape is also. African-derived nostrils are more rounded, as are many Asian-derived nostrils. Caucasian-derived nostrils and those of Hispanic peoples (which are very similar to the Caucasian skull) are more elongated. Keep in mind that this is for the majority of cases, not all. Also take into account mixed ancestry individuals perhaps not presenting with the shape you'd expect from what the rest of the skull says about ancestry. In all cases, follow what the skull tells you.

The nostrils have a direct relationship with the crista chonchalis or inferior nasal concha. According to Rynn, the top of the crista chonchalis marks the height of the nostril.

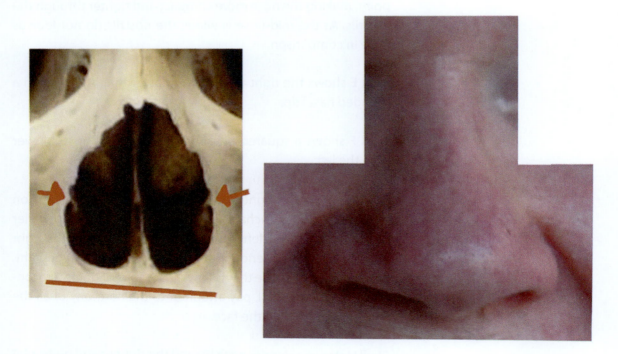

**Figure 6.25** The christa chonchalis corresponds to the top of the alar wings. Note also on this nose the width of the nasal opening and the angled inferior border. The nose in life is shown on the right.

THE NOSE 129

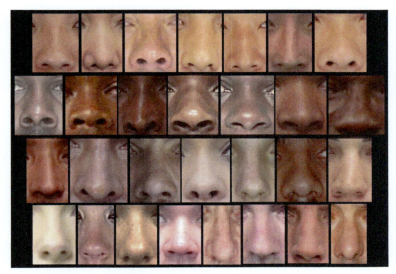

**Figure 6.26** The top row shows examples of Asian-derived noses, the second row is African-derived, the third row is Hispanic people, and the fourth row is European-derived. Notice the nostril shape, both on the inside and the outside of the nose. The inside of the Asian and African-derived nostrils are commonly rounded, Hispanic and European-derived nostrils may present more of an angled shape. Clearly this does not show every possibility of nose shape, and you can find thinner African-derived noses or wider European-derived noses. It's meant to be a selection of various shapes, and can be used for drawing practice for noses.

Nasal sills also differ according to ancestry. The excellent forensic anthropologist Dr. Kathy Taylor who worked at King County Medical Examiner's Office described them to me in the following manner:

> If you were in a tiny car driving into the nasal opening from the outside of the skull, for a European-derived nasal sill you would drive up to the edge. When you get to the nasal sill, you would go up and over the edge, and right back down inside. It is a sharp rim. For an African-derived skull, you would drive up over the edge, dip down and back up, and then go down inside. This sill is referred to as guttered. For an Asian-derived skull, you would drive up to the edge and across a flat plain, then down inside the skull.

Note this is for the base of the nasal opening only, not the sides.

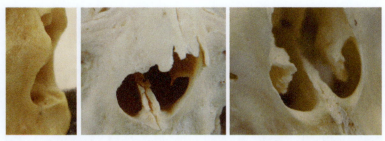

**Figure 6.27** The three nasal sills according to ancestry: African-derived is guttered, European-derived is sharp, and Asian-derived is blunt.

# Reconstruction example case

Keeping all the study info in mind, here is a nasal reconstruction with a life photo of the individual's nose.

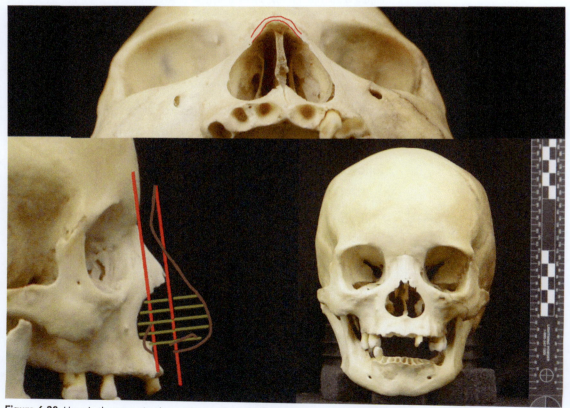

**Figure 6.28** Here is the nose tip shape, the profile with the Prokopec and Ubelaker method of nasal projection, and the skull in anterior view. The right nostril is slightly wider and higher than the left.

The piriform aperture is wide and round. The nose tip is fairly low in the opening, and widens to correspond to the nasal opening. The orbital cavities are far apart, so the nose will be wide at that location to fill the space between them. The individual is of African ancestry.

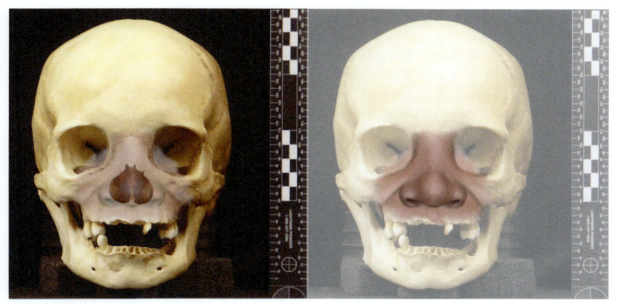

**Figure 6.29** Skull with nose overlay.

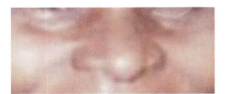

**Figure 6.30** Shows the life photo of the donor individual.

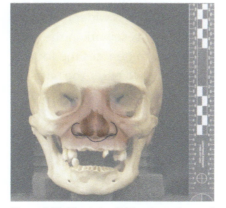

**Figure 6.31** The dark solid line shows the overlay location of the life photo of the individual. Note the photo is not a straight anterior picture, the individual is slightly turned.

Figure 6.29 shows the skull of the individual with the nose drawn on overlay. I considered the width of the nasal opening and made the nostrils 8mm wide each and rounded at the top. The right nostril flares out a little and is slightly higher than the left, matching the width of that side of the nasal opening. Note also that the nostrils direct relationship with the christa chonchalis, the structure inside the nasal opening.

This is the best life photo I have of this individual. After drawing the nose, I overlaid this photo on to my drawing to compare.

This overlay shows the correct width of the nose structure and the approximate height, taking into account the issues with the life photo. Note the rounded nostrils for this ancestry and where they attach at the top.

## More information on nose shapes

Further information regarding nose shape is noted from Gerasimov.[5] He states if the nasal aperture border is sharp, the nose is narrower relative to the aperture. If the aperture border is soft "like the opening of a shoe," the nose is wider relative to the aperture. I have not used this in my casework in the past. Additionally, he says the nasal spine form denotes the form of the nasal tip. If the spine is divided into two parts, the nasal tip will be cleft. A pointed spine indicates a pointed tip, and a broad end to the nasal spine indicates a wide heavy nose tip. This is logical and I have been using this info for many years.

# THE NOSE 133

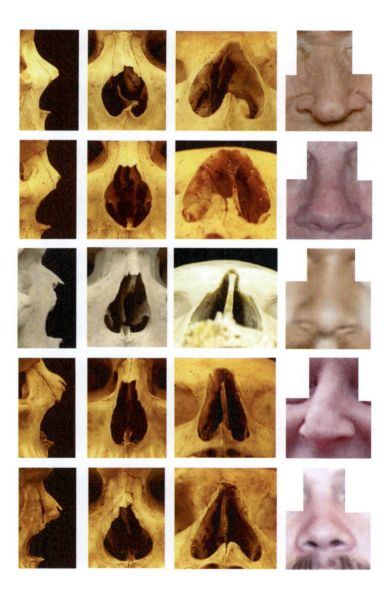

**Figure 6.32** Examples of nose shapes. Left to right are profile view, anterior view, inferior view, and life photo of each individual.

In Figure 6.32, the individual in row 1 has a bifid or lobed nasal tip. The inside of the nasal opening shows a deviated septum, which is the central vertical bone structure. The life photo shows a nose that undulates side to side, short alar wings, and a bifid tip.

Row 2 individual shows more of an oval-shaped nasal cavity. The christa chonchalis look fairly high, as this person has European ancestry. The nasal spine comes to a tip. The life photo shows a strikingly triangular-shaped nose.

The individual in row 3 is of African ancestry. The nose is not overly wide and the septum is straight. The nose leans to the left. The life photo shows an average African nose. An artist presented with this case might believe the individual to be mixed race depending on the rest of the skeletal features and develop the skin tone accordingly.

The individual in row 4 has a slender nasal cavity. The nasal spine comes to a point. In profile, the nasal opening has a shape that echoes the Roman-shaped life photo nose.

In row 5, the nasal opening is a wide teardrop shape. The nasal spine comes to a soft wide point. The life photo shows an average European nose, slightly upturned.

Each nose is unique. Pay attention to how much nostril is showing and to the shape of the nostril. On an upturned nose, the columella (the center portion of the nose where it attaches between the nostrils) may be significantly higher than the base of the nostrils. On a downturned nose, it may be much lower.

# Notes

1 Krogman, Wilton Marion, (1962) The Human Skeleton in Forensic Medicine. Charles C. Thomas.

2 Rynn, Christopher, Wilkinson, Caroline, Peters, Heather (2010) Prediction of nasal morphology from the skull. *Forensic Science, Medicine, and Pathology, 6,* 20–34. https://link.springer.com/article/10.1007/s12024-009-9124-6

3   Prokopec and Ubelaker (2002) Reconstructing the Shape of the Nose According to the Skull. *Forensic Science Communications, 4 (1).*https://archives.fbi.gov/archives/about-us/lab/forensic-science-communications/fsc/jan2002/prokopec.htm

4   Davy-Jow, Stephanie, Decker, Summer J., Ford, Jonathan M. (2012) A simple method of nose tip shape validation for facial approximation. *Forensic Science International 214* (1-3), 208.e1-208.e3.https://sciencedirect.com.science/article/abs/pii/s0379073811003781

5   Gerasimov, M. M. (1955). The reconstruction of the face from the basic structure of the skull. *Russia: Publisher Unknown*.

# 7

# CHAPTER 7

# The Mouth

*The mouth is 6 teeth wide. Vertical height is from CEJ to CEJ. Consider the age, ancestry, and sex in regards to fullness of the lips.*

While the muscles in the top half of the face mainly originate and insert into bone, many of the muscles in the bottom half insert into other muscles. This gives that part of the face much more mobility and allows you to show a great deal of expression involving your mouth. Compare on your own face how much you can move your upper face in contrast to your lower face.

All these muscles insert to the orbicularis oris (Latin for "orbiting the mouth"), a sphincter or circular muscle that surrounds the mouth and allows it to close down to protect the throat. The levator anguli oris ("elevate the angle of the mouth") raises the corner of the mouth. The zygomatic minor and major also pull the lip up. The differences in the angles where they originate gives you freedom to pull your lip up in many directions. They help you laugh and show sadness. The buccinator (trumpet) allows you to keep food on the tooth surface to eat, and to expel air as if from a trumpet. The modiolus is the fibrous structure where many of the muscles insert into the orbicularis oris.

The risorius pulls the lips straight back horizontally. The masseter allows you to open and close your mouth. The depressor anguli oris ("pull down angle of mouth") pulls down the angle of the mouth and allows you to show sadness or anger. Depressor labii inferioris ("pull down the lip underneath") depresses the lower lip. The mentalis elevates the lower lip and chin, and is the major vertical support for the lower lip.

DOI: 10.4324/9781003285588-7

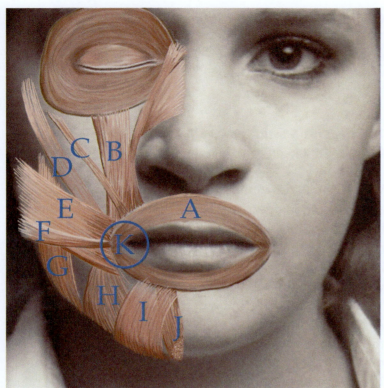

A  orbicularis oris
B  levator anguli oris
C  zygomaticus minor
D  zygomaticus major
E  buccinator
F  risorius
G  massater
H  depressor anguli oris
I  depressor labii inferioris
J  mentalis
K  modiolus

**Figure 7.1** Muscles of the midface and mandible.

The mouth area has many variables. The occlusion or malocclusion of the teeth is of great importance in shaping the lower part of the face. Occlusion refers to the alignment of the teeth, malocclusion is when the teeth do not align properly.

There are three classes of malocclusion which result in different appearances for the mouth area.

A normal occlusion is when the upper anterior teeth slightly overlap the lower teeth.

Class I malocclusion results in crowding or gaps between the teeth, or some teeth rotated. The bite can still appear normal.

Class II malocclusion occurs when the upper teeth and jaw project further forward than the lower teeth and jaw. The lower lip and chin recede.

Class III malocclusion occurs when the lower teeth and jaw project further forward than the upper teeth and jaw. The chin becomes more prominent and the lower lip protrudes further than the upper lip.

Class II is more commonly called an overbite; class III is an underbite.

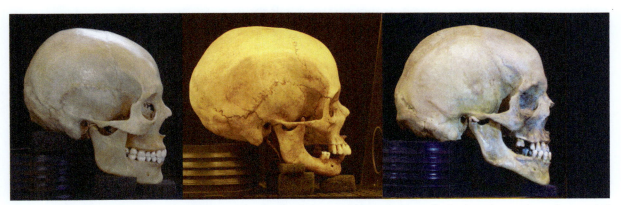

**Figure 7.2** Profile views, L to R: normal occlusion (Class I malocclusion would have similar profile lip shape but teeth may be crowded or irregularly spaced), Class II malocclusion or overbite, Class III malocclusion or underbite.

While it is a simple process to follow the layout of the mouth in profile, it is a bit more challenging to try and show the mouth with the different malocclusions in the anterior view.

# Drawing malocclusions

With a Class II malocclusion, the individual may have had trouble closing their mouth over their maxillary teeth. It can help to portray this by drawing the lips open. Depending on the size of the mandible, it may be necessary to draw a receding chin also.

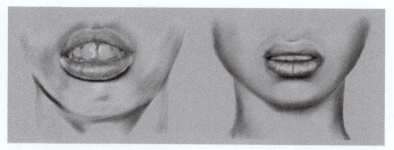

**Figure 7.3** For an overbite, often the mouth is open when it is at rest. The mandible may appear smaller than a mouth with a proper occlusion. The image on the left shows more of receding chin. The image on the right shows a smaller, more delicate mandible.

With a Class III malocclusion, the mandible projects forward and the lower lip can appear to overlap the upper lip. Consider giving the face a stubborn set to it, as though the chin is thrust forward.

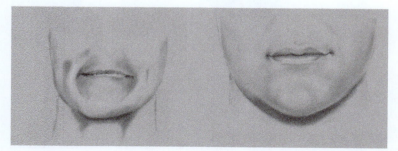

**Figure 7.4** For an underbite, the lower lip juts forward beyond the upper lip. The chin then is also more in the light than it is for an overbite. Make sure to get a good solid highlight at the furthest point of the lower lip as it thrusts forward into the light.

Albtoosh[1] found that 50% of people with a Class III malocclusion have a flat Cupid's bow.

Wilkinson[2] found the strength of the markings for levator and depressor anguli oris muscles determines whether the corners of the mouth are placed higher or lower than the commissure of the lips. Strong muscle attachments cause the bone to be uneven and rough, so compare the relative smoothness or ruggedness where the muscles attach on the zygomatic bone and mandible. Stronger attachments on the zygomatic than on the mandible indicates upturned corners of the mouth. The inverse indicates downturned. There is not always a clear difference.

## Tooth loss

A skull of someone who has lost all their teeth is called edentulous. There are two different types of tooth loss: if the teeth were lost some time before death (antemortem tooth loss), the sockets will heal over and many times it will be difficult to determine where each tooth was located. If the teeth were lost after death (postmortem tooth loss), the sockets will be clean holes that clearly delineate where each tooth was in the palate.

**Figure 7.5** Left: postmortem tooth loss. Right: antemortem tooth loss on an edentulous skull.

This will give you an idea of how to portray the individual. If the bone is edentulous, he may have appeared to have a toothless look in life. In that case, the lower part of the face appears caved in and shorter between the base of the nose and the chin. If the tooth loss is after death, the individual can be portrayed as if they still had teeth.

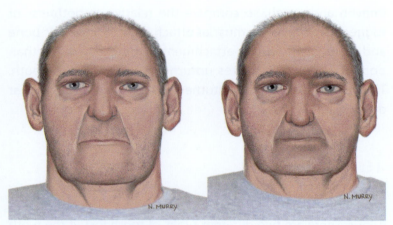

**Figure 7.6** Same skull, portrayed with full dentures and without his teeth (edentulous). The top of the head stays the same, the change is below the nose. As the bone resorbs, the space between the nose and mouth shortens and the mandible becomes less robust. The mouth gets a "caved in" look without teeth to fill the space.

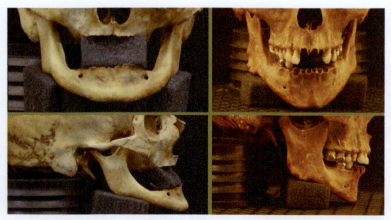

**Figure 7.7** Left: edentulous skull. Foam is placed between the cranium and mandible to estimate the space teeth would have taken in life. This step is somewhat subjective. It is possible to adjust this in your drawing software after the photos are taken. If all the bone is resorbed, the mouth should be shown with a smaller opening. This skull still shows some indication of where the teeth used to be. Notice how much smaller the mandible gets with aging. Right: skull with teeth and postmortem tooth loss. The bite can be unaffected by the tooth loss depending on which teeth are missing. If the occlusal surfaces of the molars are still intact, the bite has not changed.

Note the height of the body of the mandible and the resorbsion of the bone where the maxillary and mandibular teeth insert. On an edentulous skull where the bone has completely resorbed, the space between the nose and mouth lessens and the chin height is also shorter. See also that the missing teeth give a loss of protrusion in that portion of the mouth.

Postmortem tooth loss does not show the same qualities as an edentulous skull although both are missing teeth. A skull with postmortem tooth loss has lost the teeth after death, so the bone has not had a chance to heal over and change. The victim should be drawn as though they had a full set of teeth because that was correct in life.

## Cupid's bow

There is also specific information about the shape of the upper lip that is determined from the maxillary bone. Both Wilkinson and Albtoosh focus on the shape of the Cupid's bow, or the absence of one. Wilkinson discusses the shape of the cementoenamel junction (CEJ) of the maxillary teeth, looking for the highest points of the enamel on the central incisor. Albtoosh studied specifically the bone and tooth sockets for the maxillary incisors. She advises if the border of the bone and the maxillary teeth appears flat, the upper lip would most likely have a flat vermillion border. Wilkinson concurs and referencing the CEJ, advises if it is flat, the upper lip will be mainly flat with a negligible Cupid's bow. Albtoosh continues to advise if the border of the bone and the maxillary teeth drops down between the central incisors, the mouth will show a Cupid's bow. I have not seen this referenced in any other location but I have been comparing the skull with the life photo in several skulls and have found this seems to be the case.

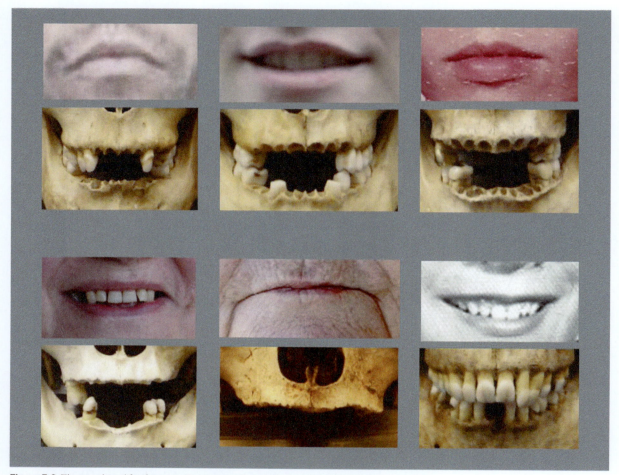

**Figure 7.8** The top three life photos and corresponding skull photos show a maxillary lip shape that includes a clear Cupid's bow. The maxillary bone dips down between the central incisors. The bottom three show a mainly flat maxillary bone line resulting in an upper lip with a negligible or flat Cupid's bow.

# Canine fossa

Another location to examine per Wilkinson is the maxillary canine fossa, the socket of the canine tooth that rises from the mouth area up towards the nose. If the skull shows a prominent definition to the fossa, she advises the upper lip should be wide and square, with a large section of maxillary teeth exposed when the mouth is at rest. In addition, a prominent canine fossa indicates a strong nasolabial fold.

# THE MOUTH

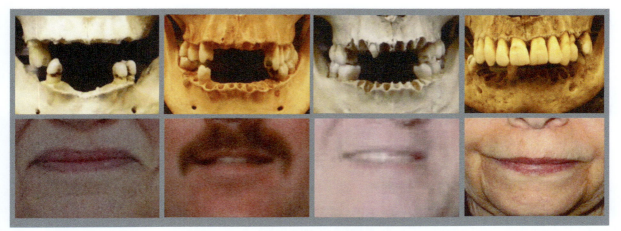

**Figure 7.9** These skulls show a maxillary canine fossa that is pronounced, like a raised tunnel above the canine tooth up towards the nose. The photos beneath each skull show that mouth in life. A prominent canine fossa indicates a strong nasolabial fold when the mouth is at rest.

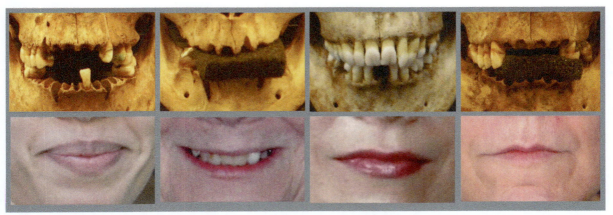

**Figure 7.10** These skulls show little or no indication of a maxillary canine fossa. The photos beneath each skull show that mouth in life. This condition should indicate a negligible nasolabial fold when the mouth is at rest. With aging and when smiling, nearly all faces will show a nasolabial fold.

This feature is age-related: those under 30 may not show as prominent of a nasolabial fold due to skin and muscle elasticity. In the case of an individual who is edentulous or merely aged, the nasolabial fold will continue past the mouth into the mandibular area when the mouth is at rest.

Some skulls show the mandibular canines or canine fossa to be prominent. Wilkinson says if that is the case, the lower lip will have a central depression and will follow the enamel line of the lower teeth.

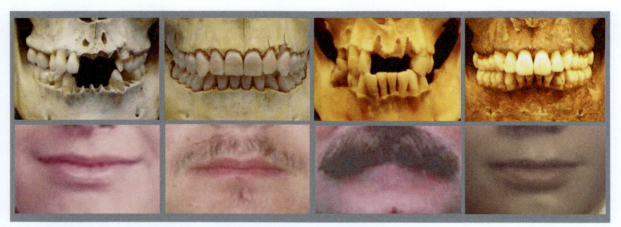

**Figure 7.11** These skulls show pronounced mandibular canines to varying degrees. The photos beneath each skull show that mouth in life.

# Philtrum

The philtrum width is associated with the mid points of the maxillary central incisors.

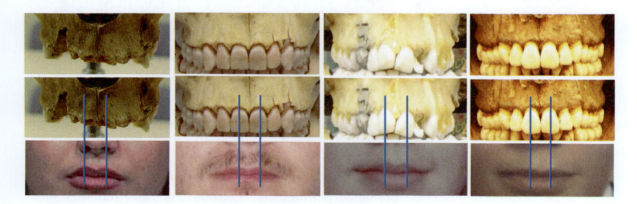

**Figure 7.12** The philtrum width matches up with the mid points of the maxillary central incisors. Top photo shows skull alone for comparison purposes, second row shows skull with mid points of the central incisors marked, last row is life photo with mid points and philtrum lined up.

THE MOUTH  149

# Infraorbital foramen

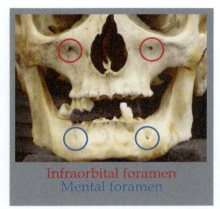

Figure 7.13 The infraorbital foramen is inferior to the orbital cavities. The mental foramen is inferior to the mandibular teeth. A foramen is a hole in the bone. Nerves pass through the bone at these locations.

In some cases, the artist has only a cranium to work with, no mandible. It can be possible that the skull is damaged or edentulous, and it may be difficult to figure out how wide to draw the mouth. One method is to use the infraorbital foramen. This is the hole in the skull below the orbital cavity that allows for passage of the artery, nerve, and vein. Dr. Song[3] and his team dissected fifty Korean cadavers to expose the infraorbital and mental foramens in order to measure where the cheilions (corners of the mouth) fell in relation to the foramens. They found that the infraorbital foramen below the orbital cavity was a good measurement to use for the width of the mouth, although they overestimate the mouth width by 0.6mm. Normally the mental foramen on the chin was medial to the cheilion and varied a good deal between ancestries, so it is not a good measurement to use for mouth width. Dr. Song advised these results seem to be similar between all ancestries and both sexes.

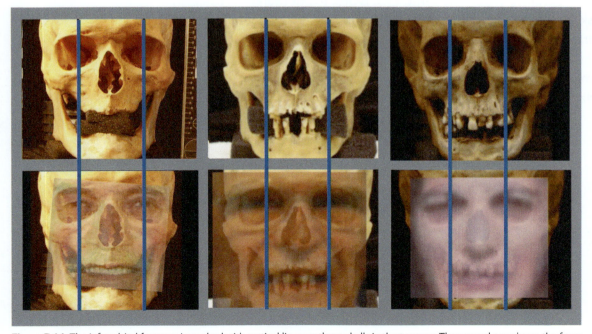

Figure 7.14 The infraorbital foramen is marked with vertical lines on these skulls in the top row. The second row shows the faces overlaid on the skulls with the same markings showing where the corners of the mouth fall on that line.

## Intercanine width

Stephan and Henneberg[4] tested the methods of mouth measurement that were used up to the time of their study in 2003. They then used photos of 93 participants and measured the width of the mouth and the intercanine width.

They found the intercanine width is 75% of the total mouth width, which allows for an easy calculation to draw the mouth. Stephan and Henneberg compared methods of estimating mouth width in 2008[5] and reported this 75% rule appears to be the most accurate. Song's method was a close second and Krogman's was inaccurate, underestimating mouth width by 7.3mm on average.

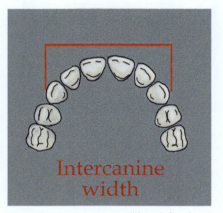

**Figure 7.15** Intercanine width is defined as the measurement from the cusp tips of the canines. Cusp tips are prominent or projecting points on the teeth. The widest point from canine to canine is indicated here as the most prominent points.

## Dentures

If the unidentified victim has dentures, it is best to photograph the skull with the dentures in place if possible so you can more accurately visualize the projection of the mouth in profile and the height of the mouth. If you cannot keep the dentures in the mouth while putting on the tissue depth markers, you can overlay them later in your software.

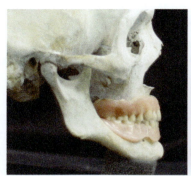
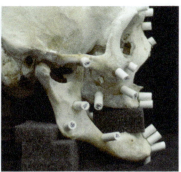
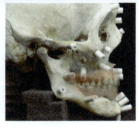

Figure 7.16 The mouth in profile with dentures placed. Tissue depth markers necessitate removal of the dentures, but it is possible to overlay them again before you do the reconstruction in drawing or photo software. The mandible can be rotated in the drawing software if the opening width estimated with foam blocks does not fit the height of the dentures.

# Notes

1 Albtoosh, Amal Aqeel Odeh (2016) Prediction of Naso-labial Morphology from Dental Pattern Assessments. University of Dundee, Doctor of Philosophy dissertation.https://discovery.dundee.ac.uk/ws/files/9137391/thesis_aalbtoosh_amended.pdf

2 Wilkinson, Caroline. (2004) *Forensic Facial Reconstruction*. Cambridge University Press.

3 Song, Wu-Chul M.D., et al. (2007) Location of the Infraorbital and Mental Foramen with Reference to the Soft-Tissue Landmarks. *Plastic and Reconstructive Surgery, 120(5),* 1343–1347.https://journals.lww.com/plasreconsurg/abstract/2007/10000/location_of_the_infraorbital_and_mental_foramen.31.aspx

4 Stephan, C.N. and Henneberg, M. (2003) Predicting Mouth Width from Inter-Canine Width – a 75% Rule. *Journal of Forensic Science 48(4)*.https://www.academia.edu/31159969/Predicting_mouth_width_from_inter_canine_width_a_75_rule?auto=citations&from=cover_page

5 Stephan, C.N. and Murphy, S.J. (2008) Mouth Width Prediction in Craniofacial Identification: Cadaver Tests of Four Recent Methods, Including Two Techniques for Edentulous Skulls. *J Forensic Odontotstomatol 27(1)*, 2–7.http://www.iofos.eu/Journals/JFOS%20June%2008/STEPHAN-MURPHY%20JFOS%20final.pdf

# 8

CHAPTER 8

# Facial Reconstruction in the UK

*Tim Widden*

Due to the lack of an internationally recognized model of best practice, regional approaches to facial reconstruction are varied. Unlike in the US, it is rare to see hand-drawn or physical 3D facial reconstructions in UK police appeals. Most reconstructions are created either as digital 3D models from which still images are exported, or 2D photographic composites.

The prominence of digital facial reconstructions in the UK has coincided with advances in 3D modelling software. One benefit of this software is the ability to observe, measure and refer back to the skull from any angle whilst building the face. The resulting realism also appears to have become a stylistic preference. However, whilst perhaps more lifelike, the fully realized, photographic results may leave less room for interpretation in the viewer and result in potential witnesses fixating on the inevitable inaccuracies rather than the broad similarities observed in a sketch or physical model.

As well as common stylistic differences between US and UK practitioners, the methods of feature approximation can also vary, some of which are described below.

## Tissue Depth

When comparing American and UK methods, one of the most striking differences is in the use of tissue depth markers. Instead of using average tissue depth data as a strict guide to locate the surfaces of the face, UK practitioners tend to use the Manchester method, which gives additional weight to the position of the underlying musculature. By observing muscle placement, the form of the overlaying soft tissues can be extrapolated.[1] This is particularly relevant to the lower face, with the position of the masseter, modiolus, zygomatic and depressor muscles contributing to the presence of convexities and concavities on the surface. The size and roughness of the muscle attachment markings on the bone are also useful for estimating the facial surface. Stronger markings suggest increased muscle volume,[2] which may indicate a divergence from what the average tissue depth data recommend. Muscle markings may also be used to predict specific facial lines, such as particularly rough procerus and corrugator supercilii attachments indicating strong horizontal nasion and vertical glabella creases. When creating a digital 3D reconstruction, the facial muscles are placed over a CT scan of the skull. For 2D photographic composites, the superficial muscles are sketched over the skull photo to guide the placement of the planes of the face.

Digital 3D reconstruction in Geomagic Freeform sculpting software, shown on right.

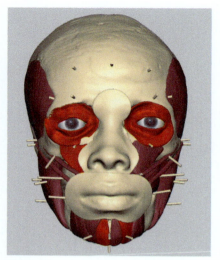

Figure 8.1 Illustration of the Manchester method, showing the skull with tissue depth markers, muscles and facial features in place.

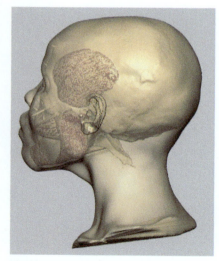

Figure 8.2 Illustration of the Manchester method, showing the skull with muscles and transparent facial features in place.

## Eyes

Whilst the overall proportions of the obits vary between individuals, a common approach in the UK is inspired by measurements by Whitnall, which showed the average eyeball to be positioned 4mm from the orbital roof, 6.8mm from the floor, 4.5mm from the lateral wall and 6.5mm from the medial wall. This places the eyeball slightly superolateral to the centre of the orbit when viewed anteriorly.[3,4]

When considering eyeball protrusion, the border of the iris is aligned with the tangent running between the anterior borders of the mid-supraorbital and mid-infraorbital margins when observed in profile view. This results in the eyeball protruding approximately 3.8mm past the tangent. Protrusion of the eyeball over the tangent can also be calculated with the equation 18.3mm − (0.4 x orbit depth).[5]

## Eyebrows

Whilst the eyebrows are generally described as following the supraorbital margins, prominent brow ridges with thick supraorbital rims indicate straight eyebrows in which the inferior border is 1-2mm below the supraorbital margin.[6]

## Ears

Whilst making an accurate prediction of the ear from the skull continues to prove problematic,[7] the following methods are commonly used for estimation. The angle of the ear to the head follows the angle of the vertical ramus of mandible.[8] The inferior border of the earlobe should also be level with the inferior border of the mastoid process.

## Mouth

Upper and lower lip thickness for male and female White Europeans and Indian subcontinent Asians are predicted from measurements of the enamel height of the maxillary and mandibular central incisors[9] using the following calculations:

White Europeans:

Upper lip thickness = 0.4 + 0.6 x maximum maxillary central incisor enamel height
Lower lip thickness = 5.5 + 0.4 x maximum mandibular central incisor enamel height

Indian subcontinent Asians:

Upper lip thickness = 3.4 + 0.4 x maximum maxillary central incisor enamel height
Lower lip thickness = 6 + 0.5 x maximum mandibular central incisor enamel height

However, dental occlusion also influences lip thickness, with greater occlusion pushing the lips forwards and outwards, thereby increasing their thickness.

# Nose

The Rynn method[10] is used to estimate nasal projection, and is used across ancestry groups and sexes. Firstly, the following measurements are taken from the skull:

X: Nasion-Acanthion (mm)
Y: Rhinion-Subspinale (mm)
Z: Nasion-Subspinale (mm)

To locate the angle of lines 1 & 2, the skull must be rotated into the Nasion-Prosthion Plane (NPP), in which the tangent running between the two points is vertical in profile view. With the skull

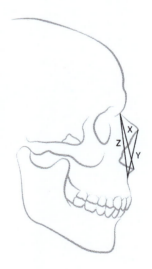

**Figure 8.3** Illustration showing the locations of the Nasion, Acanthion, Rhinion and Subspinale.

in NPP, line 1 projects horizontally out from the Nasion. Line 2 runs vertically down from where line 1 terminates. The length of lines 1 and 2 are calculated by:

Line 1: 0.83 Y – 3.5
Line 2: 0.9 X – 2

To locate the angle and position of line 3, the skull must be rotated into the Frankfort Horizontal Plane (FHP). Line 3 then projects horizontally out from the Subspinale, and is calculated by:

Line 3: 0.93 Y – 6

The box created by lines 1, 2 and 3 show the boundaries of the nose. However, to accurately estimate the nasal profile, the two-tangent method should also be incorporated. This involves drawing two lines, one following the general direction of the nasal bones and the other following the floor of the nasal aperture adjacent to the anterior nasal spine. The intersection of these lines indicates the placement of the nasal tip.

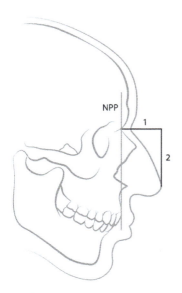

**Figure 8.4** Illustration of the skull in the Nasion-Prosthion Plane (NNP) and the placement of lines 1 & 2.

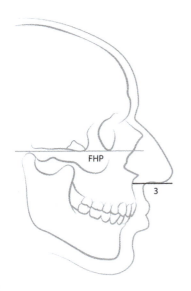

**Figure 8.5** Illustration of the skull in the Frankfort Horizontal Plane (FHP) and the placement of line 3.

## Conclusion

As research into facial approximation continues, twists and turns on the road to finding a single model of best practice are inevitable. New studies involving different sample sizes and methods may produce results that call once trusted techniques into question, or find them unsuitable for specific demographics. The vast and sometimes contradictory nature of the literature also makes the variation in approach between regions and individual practitioners unsurprising. However, by continuing to collaborate and share our practical knowledge with the global community, closing this gap is achievable.

# Notes

1 Stephan, C. (2013). *Craniofacial Identification*. Edited by Caroline Wilkinson and Christopher Rynn. Viii + 263 pp. New York: Cambridge University Press

2 Stephan, C. (2013). *Craniofacial Identification*. Edited by Caroline Wilkinson and Christopher Rynn. Viii + 263 pp. New York: Cambridge University Press

3 Whitnall, S. E. (1921) *The Anatomy of the Human Orbit and Accessory Organs of Vision*. London. Frowde and Hodder & Stoughton

4 Stephan, C. et al. (2009). *Further Evidence on the Anatomical Placement of the Human Eyeball for Facial Approximation and Craniofacial Superimposition*. Journal of Forensic Sciences. 54. 267–9

5 Wilkinson, C. & Mautner, S. (2003). *Measurement of Eyeball Protrusion and its Application in Facial Reconstruction [Technical Note]*. Journal of forensic sciences. 48. 12–6

6 Fedosyutkin, B. and Nainys, J. (1993). *The Relationship of the Skull Morphology to Facial Features*. In Iscan, M. and Helmer, R. (eds.). Forensic Analysis of the Skull. New York: Wiley-Liss Inc. pp. 199–213

7 Guyomarc'h, P. & Stephan, C. (2012), *The Validity of Ear Prediction Guidelines Used in Facial Approximation*. Journal of Forensic Sciences. 57

8 Ullrich, H. & Stephan, C. (2016). *Mikhail Mikhaylovich Gerasimov's Authentic Approach to Plastic Reconstruction*. Anthropologie (Czech Republic). 54. 97–107

9 Wilkinson, C. Motwani, M. & Chiang, E. (2003). *The Relationship between the Soft Tissue and the Skeletal Detail of the Mouth*. Journal of Forensic Sciences. 48. 728–732

10 Rynn, C., Wilkinson, C. and Peters, H. (2010). *Prediction of Nasal Morphology from the Skull*. Forensic Sci med Pathol 6, 20–34

9

# CHAPTER 9

# Traumatic Injury and Anomalies

*For a missing mandible, use artistic canons.*

Occasionally an artist will get a cranium but no mandible on a case. Babacan et al.[1] have published a study that allows the artist to reconstruct the mandible according to several measurements. Their paper shows where to make forty-eight measurements on the skull, determine six more measurements from equations using the first forty-eight, and then do a set of twenty-three complex equations to make from those forty-eight measurements in order to reconstruct the mandible in an intricate manner.

For example, to find the measurement M16, the maximum height of the mandible in the anterior view, the equation is:

$$M16 = 34.874 - (0.307 \times S16) + (0.637 \times S20) - (0.070 \times S25) + (0.453 \times S29) + (0.762 \times S37) + (0.249 \times S39) + (0.188 \times S45) + (0.174 \times S48).$$

The "S" points are the forty-eight measurements that have been previously recorded from the photos of the cranium. I do not expect there are many artists who would want to try this method, but it is available. Babacan used 3D CT images to make these measurements.

# Missing Mandible: Jefferson method

The Sassouni method has also been offered up as an option by Dr. Wilton Krogman.[2] This method requires a profile x-ray of the skull. It is somewhat complex, but Dr. Yosh Jefferson[3] has come up with a simplified way of achieving the same results. This method also requires a skull x-ray. I will give a quick demo of how to do this method if you have access to x-rays of the skull.

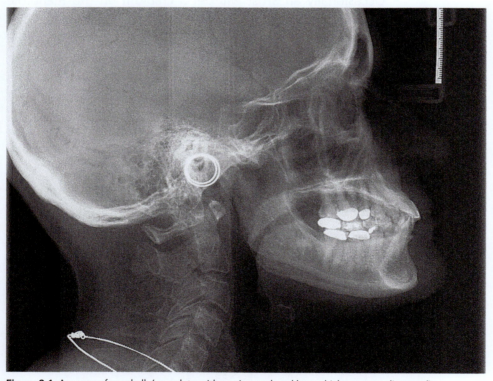

**Figure 9.1** An x-ray of my skull. (complete with earring and necklace which you may disregard).

Dr. Jefferson begins by outlining specific locations on the skull on a clear overlay on the x-ray:

The roof of the orbital cavity (an interior structure not visible on a photo of the skull)
The lateral border of the orbital cavity

The Nasion
The Sella Turcica Inferior (an interior structure of the sphenoid bone not visible on a photo of the skull)
The Anterior Nasal Spine
The Posterior Nasal Spine (an interior structure not visible on a photo of the skull)
The Pogonion (post projecting point of the front of the chin)
The Menton
Mid occlusal point of the second molar
Mid occlusal point of the second bicuspid (premolar)
Lateral border of the ramus
Inferior border of the ramus

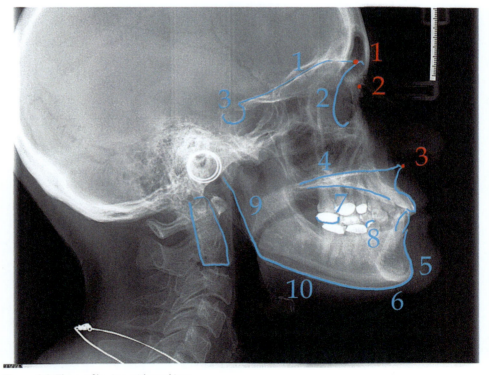

Figure 9.2 The profile view with markings.

Blue locations:

1. Roof of orbital cavity
2. Lateral border of orbit

3. Sella Turcica, inferior border
4. Posterior nasal spine (PNS)
5. Pogonion
6. Menton
7. Mid occlusal point second molar
8. Mid occlusal point second bicuspid
9. Lateral border of the ramus
10. Inferior border of the ramus

Red dots:

1. Junction of roof of orbital cavity and lateral border of orbit (called SOr)
2. Nasion
3. Anterior nasal spine (ANS)

From the tracing, you need to draw four planes:

1. Cranial plane. Draw a line connecting the SOr and the sella turcica inferior. Extend the line toward the back of the skull.
2. Palatal plane. Draw a line connecting ANS to PNS and extend it toward the back of the skull.
3. Functional occlusial plane. This line bisects the mid occlusal lines of the 2$^{nd}$ bicuspid and the second molar, and extends toward the back of the head.
4. Mandibular plane. Follow inferior ramus plane from menton toward the back of the skull.

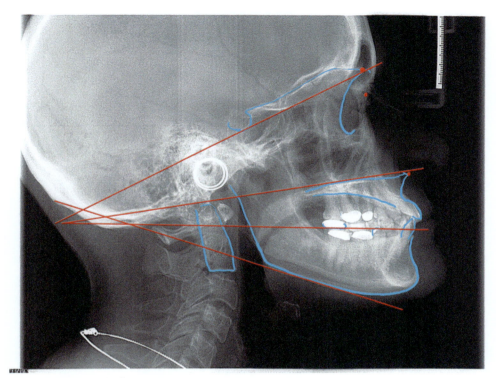

**Figure 9.3** Drawing the four planes.

After drawing the four planes, you need to locate "Center O". This is achieved by finding the smallest vertical point between the four planes where they converge. Draw a vertical line at that point, and bisect it evenly to locate Center O.

**168** READING THE SKULL

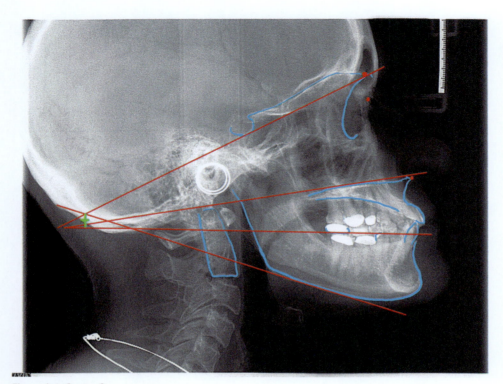

**Figure 9.4** Center O.

Next, draw an arc with the starting point at Center O, intersecting the nasion. Dr. Jefferson draws an arc but I have drawn a circle here to illustrate it more clearly.

# TRAUMATIC INJURY AND ANOMALIES 169

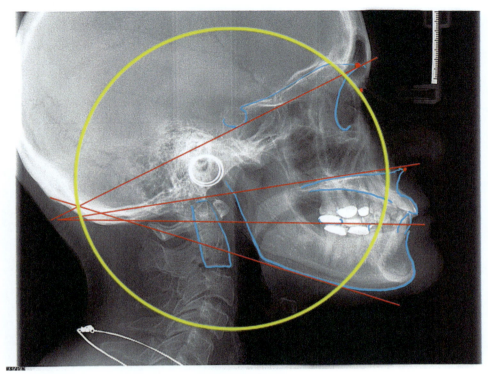

**Figure 9.5** The arc based at Center O and intersecting the nasion.

The next measurement involves drawing a circle or arc from the anterior nasal spine to the SOr (roof of the orbital cavity and lateral border of the orbit). You then duplicate the size of that circle and place it between the anterior nasal spine and the chin. In a missing mandible case, of course, there would be no chin. This second circle is the beginning of establishing where that chin would be.

# 170 READING THE SKULL

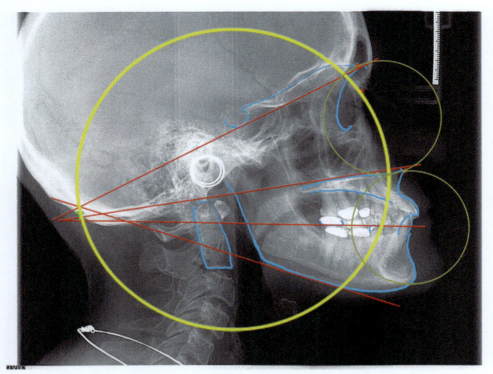

**Figure 9.6** The second set of measurements. Top green circle is between anterior nasal spine and SOr. The circle is then duplicated and moved to anterior nasal spine and chin.

After these measurements, use the ruler on the x-ray and place it beneath the second arc/circle. Draw an additional arc 10mm below the second arc/circle when doing a case for an adult. (If the missing mandible is for a child under 18, this additional 10mm measurement is not required.)

TRAUMATIC INJURY AND ANOMALIES 171

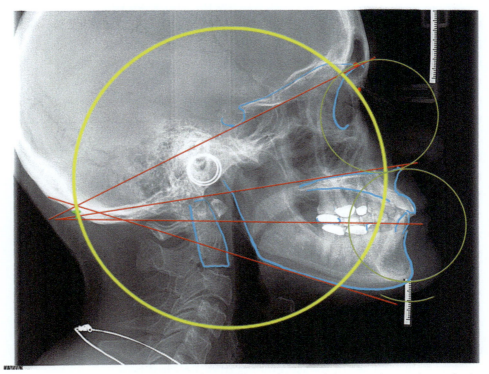

**Figure 9.7** A second arc is drawn 10mm inferior to the arc that extends between the anterior nasal spine and the chin.

This lower arc estimates the location of the chin according to divine proportions or artistic canons.

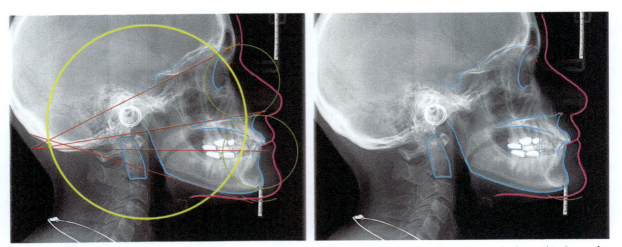

**Figure 9.8** The pink line shows the outline of my face on the x-ray. Comparing to the lower arc, this method is within 2mm of my actual chin.

As seen, this method is shown with a mandible. However, you can still get three of the four planes (all except the mandibular plane) if drawing a case with a missing mandible. It appears in most cases Center O will not be affected by not having the mandibular plane and the rest of the calculations will work. Still, most artists do not have access to a skull x-ray when working these cases. Dr. Jefferson advises matching the two anterior arcs (what I drew as green circles) results in a skull with close to divine proportions. This is important to note. This method and the Sassouni method do not figure out the size of the mandible based on the cranium. They are figuring out the size of the mandible based on divine proportions. It is not necessary to use an x-ray to use those proportions. It seems simpler to just use the divine proportions or artistic canons to get the same result, but this can be an interesting method to try if there is access to an x-ray and it is good knowledge to have.

Traditionally, artists have handled a missing mandible case by using divine proportions or artistic canons. These are basically the same thing: a set of measurements that the ideal face is supposed to fit into. Note that this is for the ideal face, not every face, but it is a good basic measurement to start with. If you do not have any information on where the chin goes, it is best to go with an average or ideal measurement

When the drawing progresses, you may find that it looks like it fits the face that is emerging better to lengthen or shorten the mandible. If it looks wrong once you have the face drawn, the mandible can be adjusted to fit that face better. It is not a hard rule that it needs to be exactly what the canons suggest. Not everyone fits into ideal proportions.

Regarding the total length of the face, the canons say it is divided into thirds: hairline to glabella, glabella to base of nose, and base of nose to chin.

# TRAUMATIC INJURY AND ANOMALIES   173

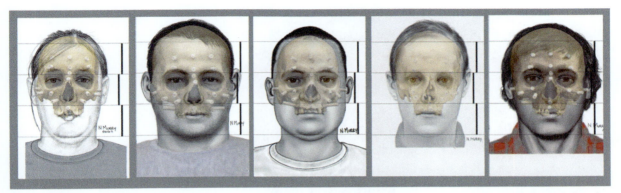

**Figure 9.9** A few cases I have drawn with missing mandibles, cranium overlaid. The thirds are shown: hairline to glabella, glabella to base of nose, and base of nose to chin.

For most cases, I have found this to be a simple method to draw a believably-proportioned face.

## Artistic canons/Divine proportions

Here are additional traditional artistic canons for the face.

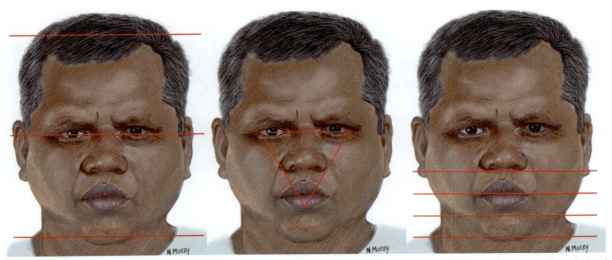

**Figure 9.10** Artistic canons state the eyes are halfway down the height of the head, the outer corners of the eyes form an equilateral triangle with the center of the bottom of the lips, and the lip line is 1/3 of the way down between the bottom of the nose and the chin.

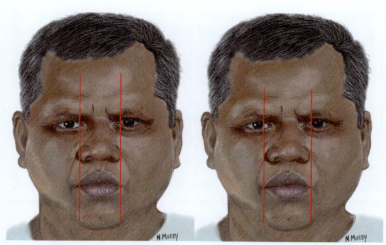

**Figure 9.11** Artistic canons state the nose width corresponds to the caruncle in the medial part of the eye and the mouth width corresponds with the inner edge of the iris.

To estimate the overall size or width of the mandible, refer to the case information provided by the forensic anthropologist. If the person had a small build, the mandible should look more delicate and slender. For a robust build, a larger wider mandible would be appropriate. Look at the mandibles in Figure 9.9 and notice the width or size of each, and how it fits in that face. See where I have placed the gonion or corners of the mandible in each case.

As stated, these are general guidelines for the perfectly-proportioned face. As you draw the reconstruction, the features may combine to make it look correct to shorten or lengthen the lower part of the face, or adjust the width. This part of the art of forensic art: using your eye to find what looks right.

# Trauma to the skull

There are cases with extensive trauma to the bone that can be completed with careful reconstruction. The following is a case I did several years ago. I was quite inexperienced with trauma this considerable at that time.

This is the skull in original condition.

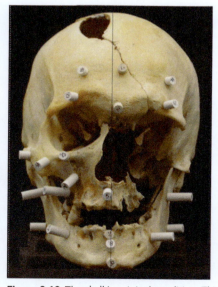

**Figure 9.12** The skull in original condition. This was early enough in my career that I did not take photos of the skull before I placed the tissue depth markers, so I do not have any photos without them. This skull shows the orbital cavity, zygomatic bone, maxillary bone, and the alveolar process on the left side extensively damaged. The damage on the top of the cranium is not important for the purposes of the drawing.

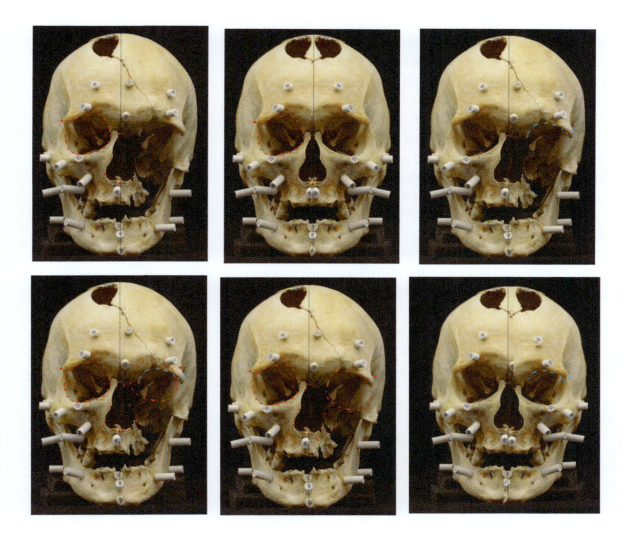

**Figure 9.13** Steps 1 through 6 in reconstructing the damaged skull.

1. I started by noting in red on an overlay some points to the undamaged right side that I would want to get correctly placed on the damaged left side.
2. Just selecting the undamaged side of the photo and flipping it over to the damaged side resulted in a skull that did not look correct. The top of the nasal bone was very thin. The whole orbital cavity area looked squashed and strange. I discarded this image.

3. I then noted in blue on an overlay some points on the damaged side that were still visible: the superior edge of the orbital cavity and a point on the piriform aperture.
4. I flipped over the overlay from the undamaged to the damaged side to see where the undamaged side lined up with the actual bone on the damaged side. It was clear that the orbital cavity needed to drop significantly, and I expected the nasal sill would also drop to match the orbital cavity.
5. I adjusted the red overlay to more closely match the blue overlay on the damaged side of the face.
6. I took the flipped undamaged half of the photo and distorted it in the software to fit the points that were visible on the damaged side. This resulted in a skull that I believe was more accurate than merely copying the undamaged side, keeping in mind a face is hardly ever symmetrical on both sides.

There may also be cases where the damage is not as comprehensive, but you may be unsure what that damage will look like on the skin level. This next case was such a case for me.

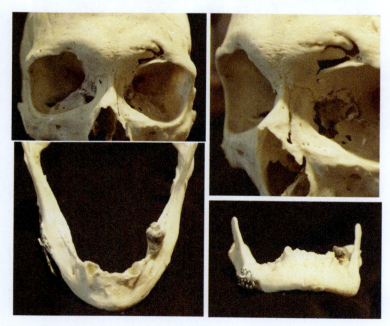

**Figure 9.14** Case with damage to orbital cavity, nasal cavity, and mandible. This individual was struck across the face at an angle, top left to bottom right.

TRAUMATIC INJURY AND ANOMALIES 177

In this case, the skull had damage above the left eye that appeared to have been from an old injury as the bone edges were not sharp and it appeared to be somewhat healed. The corresponding left side of the nasal opening was possibly injured at the same time, as there was a break to the bone. The mandible had a metal plate inserted along the inferior edge of the bone on the right side, and there was antemortem tooth and bone loss on that side of the mouth. The skull was long front to back and the nasal opening was somewhat wide, but the nasal sill was sharp. Before cleaning, the skull had retained a small patch of brown hair that appeared African-derived. It was decided this could be a mixed-race individual.

This seemed to be a traumatic injury where the victim was hit with a substantial impact across the face on an angle. My question with this was if the damage to the bone above the orbital cavity would have caused any damage to the eyeball itself or if there should have been residual mutilation to any part of the face.

I took these questions and the photos to a doctor who specialized in sports injuries and asked him to give an opinion. You might also consider a plastic surgeon, if you have or can build a professional relationship with one. I was told for this case, the eye itself should have been undamaged and thus had no changes to it. There would have been scars, but no remaining obvious wounds.

I will attach the final drawing that I came up with on this case to illustrate how I handled the injuries. Notice I thought to change the left eyelid somewhat because of the injury, and I showed scarring above that eye. As to the mandible, I kept the outline where the new plate showed it on the right side. Keeping in mind what the doctor said, I did not want to make that change too obvious or extreme. In profile, the bite looked like he could have had an underbite and he did not have any teeth, so I attempted to draw it with more of a projecting mandible as you see in someone without teeth. I did this image fairly early in my career without a lot of 2D experience, and there are many things I'd change about it now but I think it's not a bad effort.

**Figure 9.15** The image I came up with for this case.

# Anomalies on the skull

Over the years, I have found some intriguing anomalies on skulls, and I would like to share some here with you in case you come across something similar and wonder what it is. I am also of the opinion that the more you learn about the skull, the better your work can be.

This first feature is something I had myself for many years but had removed nearly ten years ago. It can be in one or both palates, maxillary and mandibular. It is called a torus or (plural) tori. They are bumps on the bone inside the mouth that grow slowly through a lifetime. They are benign and not associated with any disease or health condition. They are more common in men than women and the condition can be genetic, handed down from father to son. If they become too invasive, they can be removed by a dental surgeon.[4]

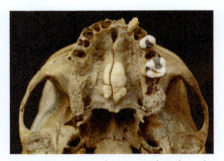

**Figure 9.16** Torus, a bony growth in the palate. This can also be in the mandibular palate, growing from the body of the mandible in towards the center part of the mouth.

Clearly this does not have any effect on the outward appearance of the mouth, but it is an interesting anomaly to the skull and it is always good to learn more about what you're working with.

Craniums have a styloid process that project from the inferior part of the temporal bone on both sides of the head. Normally, these are 2 to 3 cm long. I have come across cases where the styloid processes are much longer, and extend down into the neck.

A condition known as Eagle's Syndrome occurs when someone has extra-long styloid processes that can cause neck or cervicofacial pain.[5]

TRAUMATIC INJURY AND ANOMALIES   179

 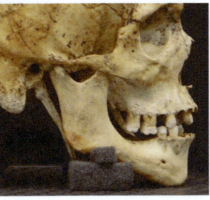

Figure 9.17 A case with extremely long styloid processes. This condition does not usually manifest on the appearance of the face and neck.

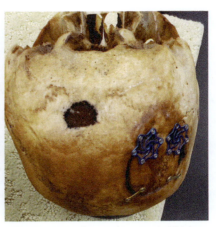

Figure 9.18 Focal avascular necrosis. This brown spot on the bone is not a hole in this cranium.

Figure 9.19 The surgery on this skull was extensive enough that it eventually resulted in the ID of this individual after photos of the skull were distributed to local neurosurgeons and one of them recognized his own work.

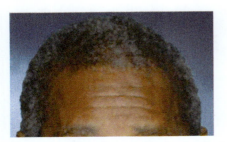

Figure 9.20 Life photo of the forehead of individual pictured in Figure 9.19.

When researching, I came across a cranium with a dark brown circular spot on the back. This was not a hole in the bone, but a spot on it. My forensic anthropologist advised that was dead bone. This occurs when the blood supply to that bone is interrupted or lost. It looks like that may have happened during brain surgery on this individual. It is called focal avascular necrosis.

The brain surgery here has cut out an access point in the bone and then metal surgical devices were screwed into the bone to hold it back together. This is not the most extensive illustration of that procedure that I have seen.

The following case has had the bone cut in several locations and has many surgical pins and screws holding it back together. These metal findings did not cause any change in the appearance of the individual.

Another anomaly that I found while researching was an extra hole behind the external auditory meatus. My forensic anthropologist advised that was mastoiditis. This is a bacterial infection that mainly strikes children. Because of antibiotics, mastoiditis is not as common as it once was.

**Figure 9.22** Post-bregmatic depression, the dip in the bone on top of the cranium.

**Figure 9.21** An example of mastoiditis. It looks like the person has two external auditory meatuses.

You may hear a forensic anthropologist refer to a post-bregmatic depression on a skull. This is commonly seen to be a trait of skulls that are African-derived.

I have seen this trait in individuals of mixed ancestry also, as long as one of the ancestries was African-derived.

The nuchal crest is a projection of bone on the back of the head. Many are fairly small but you may find a case where the bone is pulled out far enough that it is like a small ponytail on the back of the head.

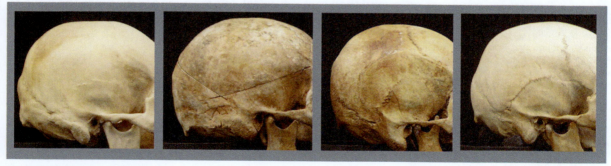

**Figure 9.23** Prominent nuchal crests.

When the nuchal crest is forming this "tail" on the back of the head, it indicates a large trapezius muscle stretched that bone out with its weight. Look for other indications on the facial bones (primarily the zygomatic bone) where the bone is lumpy

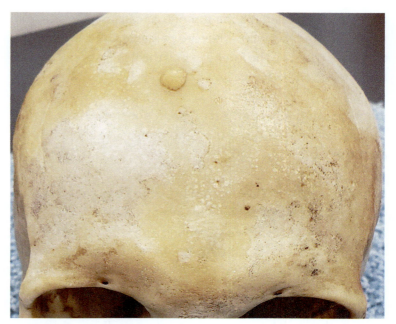

**Figure 9.24** A button osteoma.

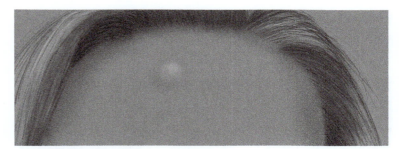

**Figure 9.25** Drawing a button osteoma.

and indicates strong muscle attachments too. Draw this individual with a heavy or muscular build. This is the same type of occurrence that you see with the Malar Tubercle in the orbital cavity where the activity of the eyelid pulls on the bone and forms the tubercle. Seeing these features on the skull shows that bone can be changed by heavy muscles or repetitive muscular activity.

While researching, I found a skull with a prominent raised lump on the forehead, like a wart of bone. This is called a button osteoma. It is a benign bone tumor that can range in size from small to quite prominent. They are palpable and can be visible especially when on the forehead or if the hair is short. They can be removed endoscopically.

When drawing a button osteoma, do not show the edges as sharply defined as they are on the bone. Give them a softer appearance.

Permanent retainers are becoming more common. This is an example of a permanent retainer in a mandible.

Whereas many of these anomalies do not have an impact on the appearance of the face, knowledge of what you are drawing always helps in accuracy. A skull that's long front to back with a post-bregmatic depression will show some African ancestry, even if the facial features themselves indicate European influence. If you draw in color, you might consider this when approaching facial tone and hair. This is not always true however, I have had cases where the skull showed strong African

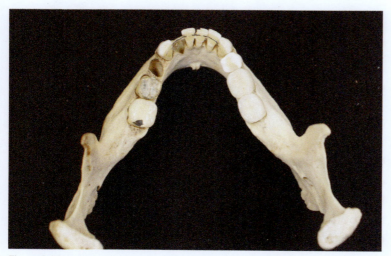

**Figure 9.26** A permanent retainer. Some are just a wire like this one, but sometimes the orthodontist adds some cement to keep it in place and to keep food from getting caught underneath the wire. This cement fuses all the teeth together on the lingual side.

ancestry but the life photo looked completely European. As in all cases, keep as open as possible in the drawing so it can be interpreted in different ways.

# Notes

1 Babacan, Serdar, et al. (2021) Redesign of missing mandible by determining age group and gender from morphometric features of skull for facial reconstruction (approximation). *Archaeological and Anthropological Sciences 13(75)*.https://link.springer.com/article/10.1007/s12520-021-01315-2

2 Krogman, Wilton Marion (1978) *The Human Skeleton in Forensic Medicine* (3rd printing). *The Use of Radiography in Skeletal Identification*. (277–299).

3 Jefferson, Yosh. (2012) *Dr. Yosh Jefferson Demonstrates his Cephalometric Analysis (part 1 and 2)*.[video], YouTube. Https://www.youtube.com/watch?v=eTMvAkAOht8 andhttps://www.youtube.com/watch?v=0Up8Uk7zUtk

4 Mermod, M., & Hoarau, R. (2015). Mandibular tori. *CMAJ: Canadian Medical Association journal = journal de l'Association medicale canadienne, 187*(11), 826.https://doi.org/10.1503/cmaj.141048

5 Gokce, Cumali, Sisman, Yildiray, and Sipahioglu, Murat. (2008) Styloid Process Elongation or Eagle's Syndrome: Is There Any Role for Eptopic Calcification? *European Journal of Dentistry 2(3)*, 224–228. https://www/ncbi.nlm.nih.gov/pmc/artices/PMC2635909/

# 10

# CHAPTER 10

# Facial Comparison

It is not uncommon for a detective or medical examiner to contact the forensic artist some time after the drawing was completed to ask for a facial comparison with a life photo of a possible match to the unknown victim. The artist can offer this service to the investigator when the drawing is released but the detective may not have good leads on the case for several years.

In many cases, the artist can only advise whether this match can be ruled out or if the investigator should continue with their scrutiny of that lead. Upon occasion, the skull anomalies are so obvious and there are enough of them that match to the life photo that the artist can advise the investigator that they believe this to be a conclusive identification. It is up to the investigator to determine if the totality of the circumstances merits an identification on the case.

Exposure over time will lead the artist to be able to differentiate between skulls and see the details that make each skull unique. This is not an easy process, made more challenging when the angle of the life photo and the angle of the skull photo do not match. If in doubt, leave the match as an open possibility.

The following will give an artist a good basic list of points to observe.

To begin, open the anterior skull photo in the drawing software, and open the life photo. Clearly it is important to get a life photo as close to a straight anterior view as possible. Driver's License photos and booking photos are usually better than candid home photos if the detective can provide that. Copy and paste the life photo on to the skull photo. Dial down the opacity on the life photo so that the skull is visible underneath. Try and fit the eyes properly in the orbital cavities. Make sure the face is slightly wider than the cranium (if you are fortunate enough to get a clear anterior view life photo) to account for tissue depth.

Observe the fit closely, taking note of each feature individually.

Check the shape and size of the cranium. Look at the shape of the mandible, and the height of the top of the head once the photo has been sized to fit the skull in most places. If the life photo is not a straight anterior view, the skull will not fit into the sides properly. The features will not fit side to side exactly, but you can compare where they are vertically on the skull: the height of the eyes, nose, mouth, and mandible. The position of where they lie on the face will still be observed. The nose must be the proper distance from the eyes and the mouth, and the width should correspond to that of the nasal cavity. The mouth to chin ratio should be the same, and the mouth width should be comparable to that on the skull. Observe the height and shape of the ears, and their position relative to the eyes and nose.

Notice specific details on the forehead, dependent on age. Look at the shape of the forehead on the skull and note where it dips and bulges. The wrinkles on the frontalis will echo this shape if the person is old enough. The prominence of the brow ridge should be noted and compared.

The eyebrows should fit along the superior rim of the orbital cavity centrally, although they may dip medially and rise laterally depending on the shape of the rim. (This is discussed further in the eye and brow chapter.) There may be asymmetry in the positioning of the brows.

The eyes should be basically centered in the orbital cavities (again, see the brow and eye chapter). They should not be too close together or too far apart to fit properly in the cavities. The corners of the eyes should correspond to the malar tubercle laterally and to the center of the lacrimal fossa medially. Check for asymmetry.

For the nose, there are a few parts to check: The width of the bridge of the nose, the body of the nose, and the base. The nostrils should be the proper width past the nasal cavity on each side, 5mm on each side for Caucasian, Asian, and Hispanic ancestry and 8mm for African. The base of the nose can be asymmetrical, and one nostril could be a different shape from the other. Asymmetry is a useful tool in this process.

The mouth should be about six teeth wide and the height of the enamel from the superior edge of the maxillary teeth to the inferior edge of the mandibular teeth. The width of the mouth can also be compared to the infraorbital foramen. If the victim is older, the vermillion could be less full. Check the edge of the maxillary bone and teeth and see if the bone dips between the central incisors, indicating the victim had a Cupid's bow. Look at the size of the philtrum. The midpoint of one maxillary central incisor to the other indicates the width of the philtrum. The dentition and occlusion on the skull should correspond to the shape of the mouth on the life photo. Observe the prominence of the canine fossa to determine if there should be a strong nasolabial fold.

The chin and jawline shape and prominence should be compared. If the person is somewhat heavy, the jawline may be less defined but the shape and location of the chin will be correct. Note where the gonion is, where the shape of the body of the mandible turns to form the ramus.

The *Handbook of Craniofacial Superimposition*[1] gives a list of several locations on the skull in both anterior and profile views that can be helpful to pay attention to when attempting a comparison. The following image illustrates a number of these

**190**    READING THE SKULL

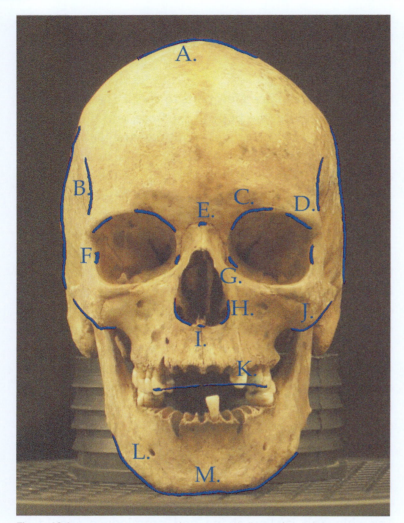

**Figure 10.1** Locations to note on the anterior skull view for skull-face craniofacial superimposition.

points to be aware of when examining the skull in preparation to comparison.

The points noted on the image:

A. The general outline of the head. The face in the life photo must be slightly larger than the bone to account for tissue depth.

B. The temporal line. The change of plane from front of the face to side of the face can often be seen on the life photo.
C. Medial part of supraorbital ridge. The medial portion of the eyebrow should correspond to this location. If there is a brow ridge, the eyebrow will be below this edge.
D. Lateral part of supraorbital ridge. The eyebrow should correspond to this part of the orbital cavity, skimming along the edge or rising higher, depending on the rest of the orbital cavity and brow formation.
E. Nasion. Directly below the glabella, where the frontal and nasal bones meet. This corresponds to the root of the nose.
F. Whitnall's or malar tubercle. The lateral eyelid must attach at this location.
G. Lacrimal fossa. The medial eyelid attaches here. It is debated where upon the fossa the attachment falls (the top, halfway down, a mm measurement from the top) but there needs to be a relationship from the eye in life to this location.
H. Width of piriform aperture. The nasal opening is 3/5ths of the total width of the nose. The nostrils make up the other 2/5ths.
I. Nasal spine. This corresponds to the tip of the nose on the life photo.
J. Zygomatic arch. This will have a relationship to the midface and cheekbones seen on the life photo.
K. Occlusal line. This corresponds to the lip closure line on the life photo.
L. Mandibular outline. This directly corresponds to the life photo, depending on the weight of the subject. A heavier person will not have a clear mandibular outline.
M. Mental outline. The chin outline will follow the mental outline on the bone.

If the artist has access to a profile photo, they can observe additional points.

The points noted on the image:

**192** READING THE SKULL

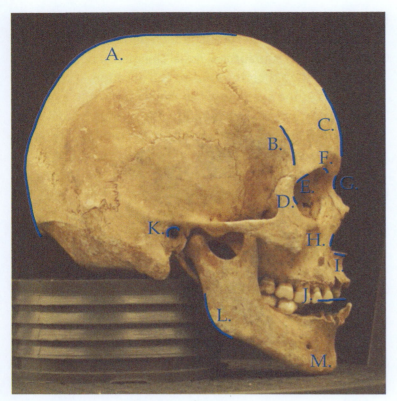

**Figure 10.2** Locations to observe in profile view.

A. General outline of the skull. This must correspond to the head shape, with the addition of tissue depth accommodation.
B. Temporal line. This location can be observed on the profile view in some individuals.
C. Frontal bone contour. The forehead in the life photo should correspond to this contour.
D. Whitnall's tubercle. The lateral eyelid will attach here.
E. Lateral part of supraorbital margin. Shows lower edge of lateral part of the eyebrows.
F. Medial part of supraorbital margin. This shows the upper edge of the medial portion of the eyebrows.

G. Nasion. This should be higher than the root of the nose, which is just below it, to accommodate for tissue depth.
H. Edge of piriform aperture. This will be posterior to the edge of the alar.
I. Inferior border of piriform aperture. This will be the alar baseline.
J. Occlusal line. The occlusal line corresponds to the lip closure line in life.
K. External auditory meatus. This will be lateral to the upper edge of the tragus on the same horizontal plane.
L. Gonial outline. Corresponds to the jaw outline in life.
M. Mental outline. Corresponds to the chin in life.

The following three images illustrate how to do a basic skull to photo comparison. Each image of four photographs is divided in this manner:

Top left: the skull. Top right: notations on a separate layer showing where features will be located. Bottom left: the life photo. Bottom right: life photo with the skull locations marked.

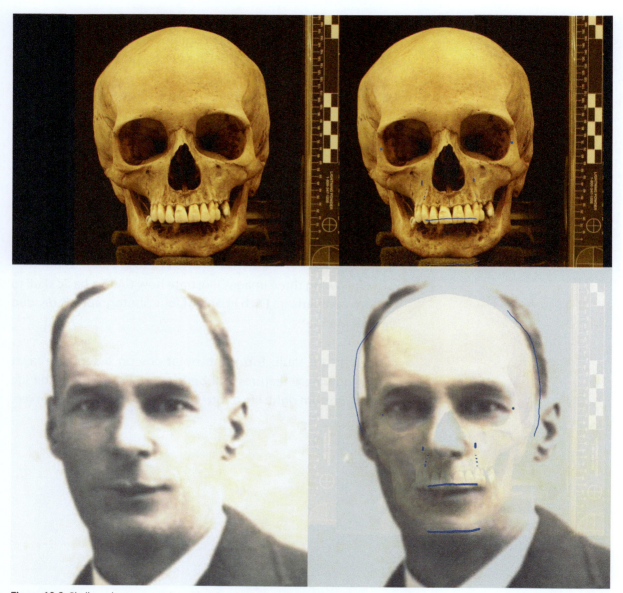

**Figure 10.3** Skull to photo comparison #1. When looking at the orbital cavities on the skull, the left side cavity rises higher than that on the right. The face in this does not echo that. The Whitnall's tubercle on the right eye is too low for this individual. The piriform aperture indicates a wider nose than this individual possesses. I have also outlined the maxillary canine fossa on the skull, they do not line up properly with this face. The fossa and the rest of the bone give the upper mouth region a more square appearance that this face does not show. His nose is slightly higher than the piriform aperture would indicate. His mouth is too low and his chin is much lower than the chin of this skull. The skull shape itself is more rounded, while this individual has a longer head. This individual would not be a match to this skull.

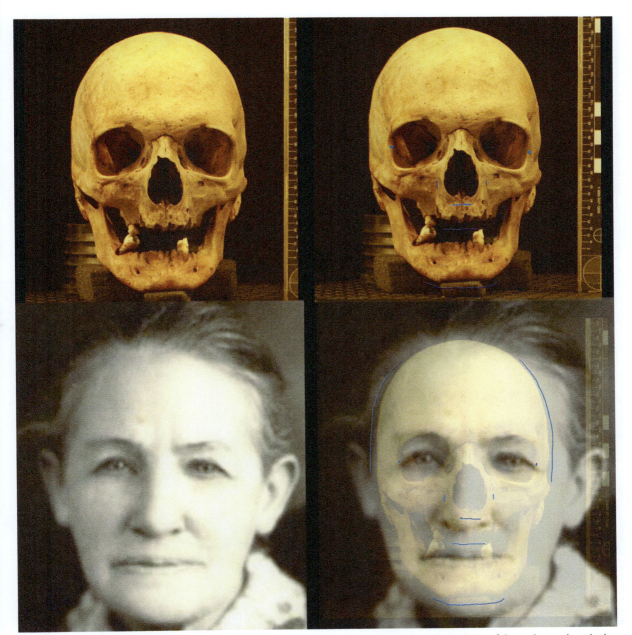

**Figure 10.4** The Whitnall's tubercles on this skull match up fairly well with this individual. Notice the shape of the eyebrows though: the left eyebrow follows the supraorbital rim and the right eyebrow does not. The glabella indicates a stronger brow ridge than this individual seems to possess. The piriform aperture is somewhat slender and even throughout the length, this individual's nose is wider at the base/nostrils than than the aperture would suggest, and the nose is too low on the face. The mouth is also lower than the lipline would indicate on the skull, and the chin is too low. The top of the ears on this individual protrude, but the skull rises smoothly on either side without any protrusion. This individual would not match this skull.

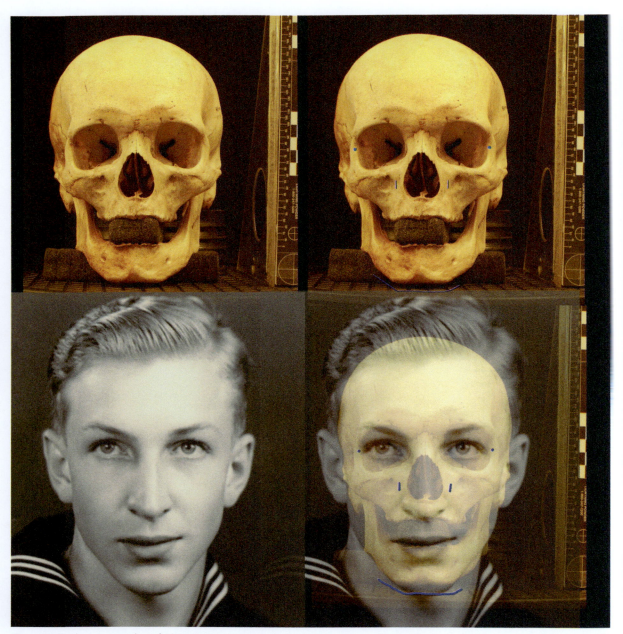

**Figure 10.5** The eyes match up fairly well with this skull. The skull shows a strong brow ridge that seems heavier than that on the life photo of this individual but a profile photo would show that better. The width of the nose in the life photo seems a bit slender for the width of the piriform aperture, and the tip of the nose is far too low. The mouth is extremely low no matter how the mouth of the skull is adjusted for the lack of teeth. The shape of the mandible appears too wide for the mandible of this individual and the gonions do not match up with the "corners" of the mandible on the life photo. This individual would not be a match to this skull.

These examples are done with clear anterior photos although the lighting is not optimal in all of them. It is not always the case that you would get such good comparison photos. The person could have their chin lifted or lowered, or the photo could show them in a three-quarter view.

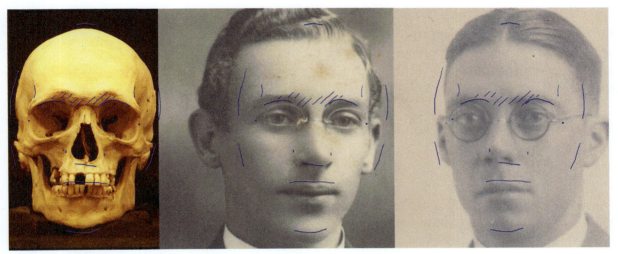

**Figure 10.6** Facial comparisons with less-than-optimal life photos.

Both individuals were photographed on an angle. I have also rotated both photos from the original provided so that the eyes are more level. The blue measurement lines from the skull photo have been overlaid on both life photos.

Match 1 (in center) show the eyes fairly well placed in this skull. The nose seems to fit well although the piriform aperture on this skull is uneven: high and wide on the right, low and slender on the left. It is possible this individual has that anomaly also but it is not completely clear with this angle. The mouth is extremely low for this skull. The width of the cranium looks like it might match although I question the width of the mandible.

Match 2 (on right) The eyes on this skull also fit in the orbital cavities. The nose looks too thin for this head. The mouth is also too low on this individual for this skull. The head seems to be about the correct width.

Note the noses on these individuals are different from each other in the direction they are "pointing." If you had taken profiles photos of this skull, you could check the nasal spine and the profile view of the piriform aperture to see where the tip of the nose should be. The Whitnall's tubercle looks higher on the right than the left on the cranium. Photos taken at slight angles make it difficult to see if the individual has that same feature.

Neither of these individuals would be a match to the skull, most clearly because of the location of the mouth in each of them.

For many cases, this is as specific as an artist should get. There are times though where enough details are visible on the skull that correspond to those on the life photo where a more definite ID will be possible. The following case study was originally published as "Skull-to-Photo Comparison for Identification Purposes" in the *Journal of Forensic Identification*, 2021, 71 (2). I have made some changes to the article for this book.

In early 2020, I was asked to assist on an unidentified remains case. In this case, the Medical Examiner had one victim of a house fire who was unidentified. The home owner was the probable victim but the ME was unwilling to sign off on the victim without further confirmation of identification. There was no living family to compare DNA, no dental records to compare, and no medical records. They asked that I do a skull to photo comparison to possibly assist in adding to the preponderance of evidence that this was their homeowner, or to rule this person out as the victim.

I was given the Driver's License photo of the possible victim before I viewed the skull, and I examined it in order to see if the subject had any identifiable features that I would want to look for on the skull when I examined it at the ME's office.

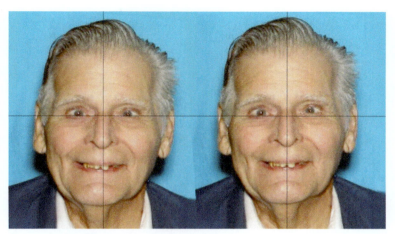

**Figure 10.7** Drivers License photo of the possible match. Lefthand view shows the eyes leveled, righthand view shows the skull itself leveled. I chose to use the view where the eyes were leveled. When I examined the skull later, the orbital cavities were level in the head.

The DL photo presented some challenges in that the subject's face was not level and was not symmetrical. Without bony landmarks, it was a somewhat subjective exercise to level the face. Additionally, the subject had an asymmetrical smile that pulled up all the features on the right side of his face. I used the eyes as a landmark to level the face. I am aware that the head appears tipped in this view, but it does match the skull when I overlay the two later. The important point is to match the angle of the life photo to the angle of the skull photo.

I observed asymmetry in the right side of his face, most notably in the lower fleshy portion. His mandible was fuller on the right side but I could not say how much of that buccal fullness was due to his crooked smile. I saw though that his maxillary central incisors were crooked (each of them tipping out laterally) and off center of the midline of his face. If his teeth were still intact, it should be fairly easy to match those. He had a missing maxillary lateral incisor. His right ear was also considerably higher than his left by about 5 mm. His chin appeared wider on the right than on the left. His nose is crooked and the right nostril is lower and wider than the left.

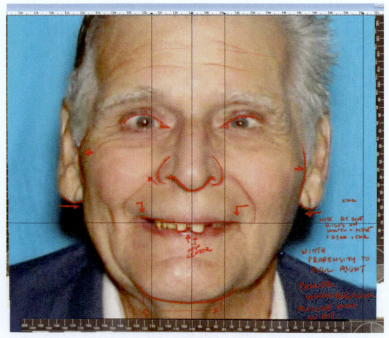

**Figure 10.8** DL photo notes with guidelines. This shows the difference in heights in ear lobes, the maxillary central incisors off center of midline of the face, and the chin off center of the face. I also noted the buccal area of the right side of the face was fuller, but I was unsure if this would be visible on the skull and if it was due to the propensity of the face to pull up to the right.

When I went to the Medical Examiner's Office, I found that the skull was not damaged by fire but none of the maxillary incisors were remaining. The maxillary canines were still in the skull but were damaged. I photographed the skull from both profiles and the anterior, and additionally photographed an inferior view of the maxillary teeth and palate. I later arranged the profile and anterior photos and sized them in a layout to view all three views in a panorama in my drawing software.

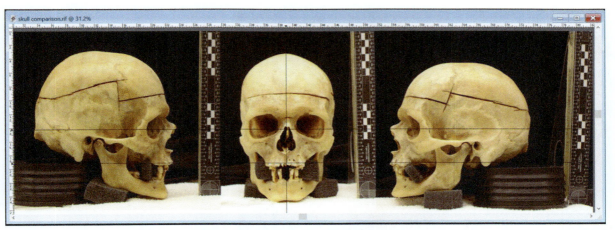

**Figure 10.9** Panorama of skull photos: right profile, anterior, left profile. Guidelines used to line up features on the horizontal for all three photos and one on the midline on anterior photo.

When I had all three photos arranged, I placed a clear layer over the anterior photo and drew an outline of the skull.

Once I had the basic measurements on the skull, I brought in the inferior view of the maxillary palate to confirm I had correct placement of the maxillary teeth. I was able to line up the palate with the remainder of the canines using vertical guides. Note in this view that there is breakage to the maxillary bone where the teeth insert, but the palate gives a clear indication where the teeth are placed. The guides on my image are lined up to the outer edges of the canines. A portion of the first pre-molar #12 is visible behind the canine on his left side, not to be confused with the canine. This view shows clearly that the central incisors midline (indicated with the green measurement marking) is to the right of the facial midline (indicated with blue guideline).

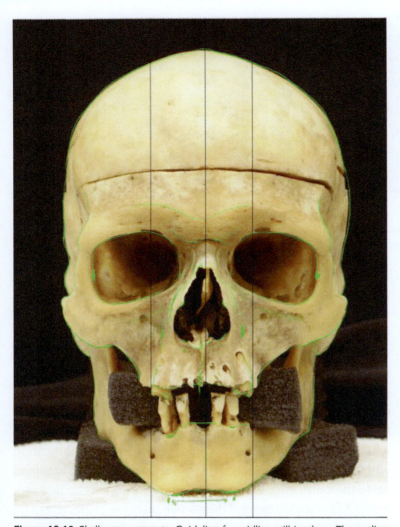

**Figure 10.10** Skull measurements. Guideline for midline still in place. The outlines in green are my notes, especially showing the off-center placement for the maxillary central incisors and the crooked chin. I am noting here also the malar tubercles for eyelid placement. I show the brow ridge, the zygomatic bones, where the width of the nostrils should fall, the right nostril being lower than the left, and the asymmetrical mandible.

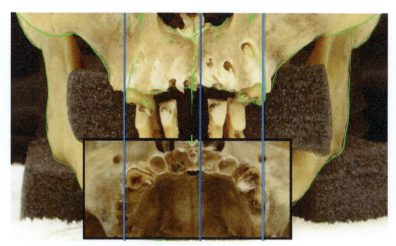

**Figure 10.11** Lining up the maxillary palate. Lateral sides of canines of skull in anterior view lined up with lateral sides of canines on the palate in inferior view. The midline of the central incisors is then visible as indicated by the green arrow.

After determining the layout of the skull, I brought in the DL photo of the possible victim and sized it over the anterior skull photo. I did not put tissue depth markers on the skull at the ME's office since I was not doing a reconstruction, but I sized the DL photo to what I felt was the proper size to this skull, allowing for tissue depth on all sides and fitting the eyes into the orbital cavities.

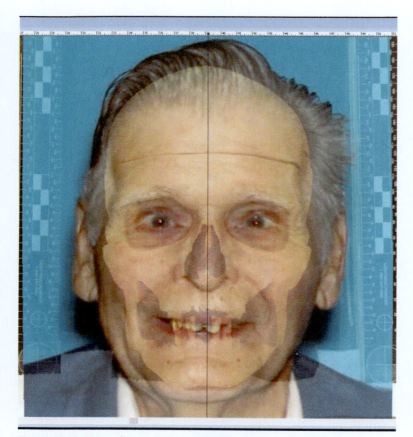

**Figure 10.12** DL overlay on skull, opacity of DL photo turned down to view skull beneath.

Upon placement of the DL photo, initial assessment showed the general fit to be a good one. Eyes were fairly centered in the orbital cavities allowing for slight changes due to photo angle. Eyebrows followed the superior edge of the orbital cavity. The nose fit into the nasal cavity properly. The zygomatic bones and mandible fit into the head properly. With the tooth loss, I was unable to match up the dentals easily at first. I turned on the view of the palate and the skull measurements over the DL photo.

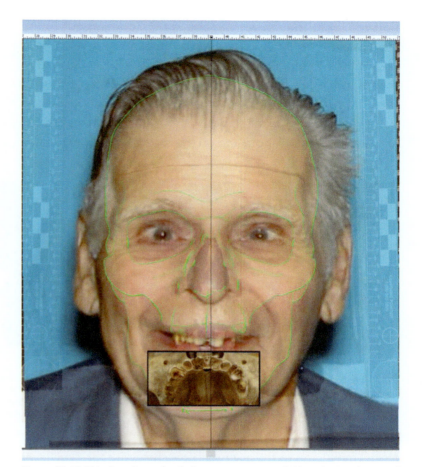

**Figure 10.13** This view shows the skull measurements overlaid on the DL photo, and the inferior view of the palate over the DL photo. This confirms the subject's maxillary central incisors match up with the skull palate and shows the bone structure over the DL photo. Notice also the asymmetry to the inferior edge of the zygomatic bones. I do not know if the thickness of the righthand bone contributes to the thickness of the muscles on that side of his face or if that is due to the lopsided smile. If, as his life photos suggest, he always smiled on the right side of his face, he could have built up the buccal muscles on that side of his face more and they may have built up the muscle attachment on the zygomatic bone slightly. Conversely, the zygomatic bone could have been more robust on the right than the left from birth, causing the asymmetry to his smile.

With the palate view turned on, the teeth lined up with the DL teeth confirming again that the off-centered incisors for the subject and the skull matched. Because the possible victim did not have dental records, it is unknown the state of his teeth prior to his death. There is another DL photo taken after this one (but at a slight sideways and downward angle and with a closed mouth) that appears to show him more edentulous.

I moved on to the uneven earlobe issue. Zooming out to the view of all three skulls, I drew horizontal lines at the superior edge of the external auditory meatus on each profile and at the inferior edge of each earlobe on the life photo. Lines for the right ear are in red and for the left ear are in purple. As can be seen in Figure 10.14, the right ear is clearly higher than the left, both on the DL photo and on the external auditory meatus of the skull.

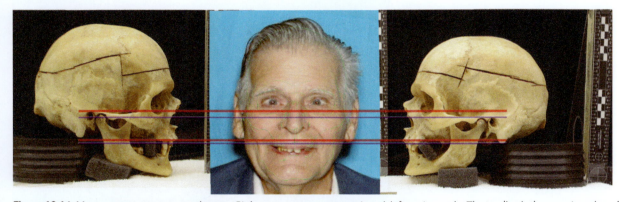

**Figure 10.14** Measurements to compare the ears. Right ear measurements are in red, left ear in purple. The top line is the superior edge of the external auditory meatus on the skull photos, the bottom line is the inferior edge of the earlobe on the life photo. These measurements show the right ear is clearly higher in both the life photo of this subject and on this skull. Note that the base of the earlobe corresponds to the tip of the mastoid process. The mastoid processes are downward-directed, and the ears in the life photo are ambiguous.

Next, I moved on to the asymmetrical chin. With the skull layer turned on, I moved the ruler below the mentalis and centered the 100mm mark of the ruler on the midline. I observed the most prominent point on the right side of the mandible to be about 17mm lateral of the midline, and about 13mm lateral on the left.

**Figure 10.15** An earlier life photo of this individual appears to show an attached earlobe.

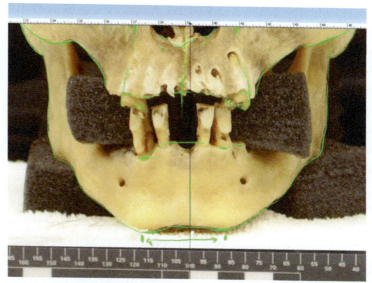

**Figure 10.16** Mentalis midline on the skull, measuring most prominent points on either side of the chin. The right side of the chin extends further than the left.

When turning on the DL photo layer, I repeated the same measurements. On this layer, the right side of the chin's most prominent point was about 30mm off center and the left side was about 18mm off center.

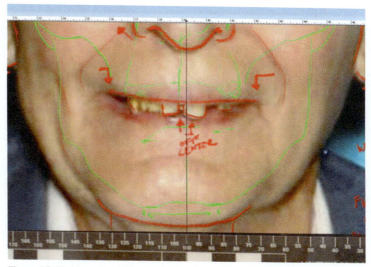

**Figure 10.17** Mentalis midline on the DL photo, measuring the most prominent points on either side of the chin. The right side of the chin extends further than the left on both the skull and the life photo.

To conclude, the entire head shape fit onto the skull with no glaring issues that would cause concern. If I were presented with the photo of the skull and the DL photo, I would not be able to rule this person out as a possible match. But when examining both the skull and the photo in greater detail, I found the anomalies of this individual that were present in both the DL photo and the skull were the asymmetry of the ears, the off-center maxillary central incisors, and the asymmetry of the chin. The shape of the nose also contributed to individualize this skull.

Considering an elderly Caucasian male was found deceased in this man's home after a housefire, I would determine the chances of this individual being anyone other than the homeowner to be extremely slim. After presenting my findings to the Medical Examiner, she was comfortable closing the case based on the preponderance of the evidence.

Doing a skull to photo comparison is not something that an artist usually does on a regular basis and it is challenging to find any instruction or specialists in this subject. Proceed with caution and do not attempt to definitively identify anyone as a match without several individualizing points on the head. Often just ruling someone out or in is helpful to the detective on an unidentified remains case.

# Note

1 Damas, Sergio, Cordon, Oscar, and Ibanez, Oscar. (2020) *Handbook on Craniofacial Superimposition, The MEPROCS Project.* Springer. https://doi.org/10.1007/978-3-319-11137-7

# Index

*Note*: Figures are shown in *italics* and tables in **bold type**.

75% rule, for estimating mouth width 150
3D modelling software 155

abnormalities 22, 29–30
acanthion *106*, 107
African Americans 92–4, 127
African ancestry 86, *93*, 103, 128, *129*, 129, *130*, 131, 134, 177, 180, 182–3, 189
aging 75, 91, 95–6, *144*, *147*
alar wings *128*, 133
anatomical terms of location 8
ancestry 5, 9, 15, 72, **110**, 128–9, 132, 139, 180; African *see* African ancestry; African American 127; Asian 82, 84, 131, 189; Asian/Native *65*; Caucasian 189; European 84, 86, 111, 131, 134; Hispanic 189; mixed 180
anomalies 22, *24*, *126*, 178–83
ANS (Anterior Nasal Spine) 159, 165, 166, 169, *170*, *171*
antemortem tooth loss 27, *28*, 44, 66–7, 143, *143*, 177
anterior drawing *24*, 104
anterior lacrimal crest *79*
anterior life photo 38, 187, 188, *196*, 197
Anterior Nasal Spine (ANS) 159, 165, 166, 169–70, *170*, *171*
anterior skull photo 9, 103, 104, *130*; face and ears 37–8, 41, 42, *46*, *46*, 51; facial comparison 187, 189–90, *190*, *196*, 196–7, 200, *201*, 201, *203*, 203; photographing the skull 13, 16, 17, *17*, 18, 22, 30, *30*

aperture priority 19–20
APS-C sensors 18–19, 21, *22*
Armstrong, Gerald *63*
Arneson, Richard *56*
artistic canons 163, 171, 172, 173, *173*
ArtStudio Pro *6*
Asian ancestry 82, 84, 130, 189
Asian eyes 96, *96*
Asian-derived noses *129*
Asian/Native ancestry *65*
asymmetry 24, *30*, 31, *52*, 70, 188–9, 199, *205*, 208; *see also* symmetry
attached earlobes 39, 41, *41*, 42
average ears 37, *37*
average lateral supraorbital rims 88, *89*

background, for photographs 16, 19–20
Bomberry, Daniel Robert 67, *67*
bones 8; facial 181; nasal 127, 159, 191; temporal 40; zygomatic 29, *58*, *60*, *62*, *63*, 70, 71, *201*, 204, *205*
brow 5, 75–97
brow ridge 22, 23; case work 55, *58*, *59*, *60*, *62*, *63*, 64, *65*, 66, 68–9; eye and brow, *82*, *84*, *85*, 85, 86, *86*, 88, 88, *89*, 89; facial comparison 188, 191, *195*, *196*, *201*
buccinator muscle 139
button osteoma 181–2, *181*

cameras 14, *17*, 18–21, *22*
canine fossa 28, *28*, *60*, *61*, *62*, 67, 146, *147*, *147*, 189, *194*
case work 55–72

cavity: nasal 44, *46*, 103, 134, *176*, 188, 189, 204; orbital (*see* orbital cavity); supraorbital *82*
cementoenamel junction (CEJ) 139, 145
central incisors 47, *58*, 145, *146*, 201, *203*; maxillary 55, *61*, 66, 67, 147, *148*, 158, 189, 199, *200*, *201*, *205*, 208
chin 44, 47; case work 60, *62*, 64–5, 69, 70; facial comparison 188, 189, 192, *194*, *195*, 197, 199, *200*, *201*, 206, *207*, 207, *207*, 208; mouth 139, 141, 142, *142*, 143, 145, 149; traumatic injury and anomalies 165, 169, *170*, 171, *171*, 172, *173*
Class I malocclusion 141, *141*
Class II malocclusion 141, *141*, 142, *142*
Class III malocclusion 141, *141*, 142, *142*
Conrad, Timothy *59*
Corel Painter 5, *6*
corrugator supercilii muscle 75, *75*, 91–2, 156
cranial plane 166
cranium 5, *144*, 149, 188, 197; case work 58, *59*, *61*, 70, 71; face and ears 38, 38–45, *46*; *photographing the skull* 16, 17, 23, 28, 29, *29*, 30, *30*; *traumatic injury and anomalies* 163, 172, 173, *174*, 179, *180*
crista chonchalis *57*, 128
Cupid's bow *55*, 68, 142, 145, *146*, 189
curved brow *97*

deepset eyes 89, *89*
dentures 27, *60*, *144*, 150, *151*
depressor angular oris *140*
depressor labii inferioris 139, *140*
depth of field 20
depth of focus 20
digital drawing software 5–6
digital facial reconstruction 141
distance between medial canthi (DMC) 75, *76*, 95
divine proportions 171, 172
DMC (distance between medial canthi) 75, *76*, 95

double eyelid crease 93, *93*
downward-directed mastoid process 35–36, 39
drawing lines to compare symmetry *47*

Eagle's Syndrome 178
ears 35–52; lobes 35, 39, *200*; *UK approach to the* 201
edentulous skull 27, 28, *28*, *60*, 143–4, *142*, *144*, 147, 149, 205
edge of piriform aperture 193
epicanthic fold 82, *85*
European ancestry 84, 86, 111, 130, 134
European-derived noses 129, *128*, *129*
exposure 19–20
external auditory meatus *17*, 36, 38–9, *105*, 179, *180*, 193, 206, *206*
eyeball 75, 76–81, *77*, *78*, 90, *91*, 156–7, 177
eyeball protrusion 80
eyebrows 6–7, 23, 75, 81, 85–8, *88*, 184; height 92, 93, 95; shapes 59, 85–8, *86*, *88*, 95–6, *96*, *97*, *195*; *UK approach to* 157
eyelids *60*, 90, *91*, 91–3, *93*
eyes 23, *55*, *60*, *62*, 69, 75–97, *173*; Asian *96*, 96; deepset 89, *89*; and facial comparison 188–9, *196*, 197, 199, *199*, 203, 204; UK approach to 156–7

facial approximation 159
facial bones 180–1
facial comparison 187–208
facial harmony 43–4, *44*, *45*, *46*
facial plane 17, 20, 23, *24*, 29, *29*, 30, 38–9, 41, 43, 90, *91*
facial reconstruction, in the United Kingdom 155–9
feature approximation 155–9
females 23, 35, *68*, *71*, **110**, 111, 157–8; eye and brow 80, 89, *89*, 91–6, *96*
Ferguson model 44U-305 flexible pipe fitting adapter 16
FHP (Frankfort Horizontal Plane) 15, 16, *17*, *23*, 105, *105*, 111–12, 120, *120*, 159, *159*

fissure slant 93, *93*
flaring ears *42*
foam 14, *14*, 15, 15, 16, *17*, 17, *151*, *151*
focal avascular necrosis 179, *179*
focal length, of camera lens 13, 18, 19, 20, 21
forehead *58*, *90*, 91, *179*, 181–2, 188, 192
*Forensic Art and Illustration* 4
*Forensic Facial Reconstruction* 4
forward-facing mastoid process 35–6
framing square 16, *17*
Frankfort Horizontal Plane (FHP) 15, 16, *17*, *23*, 105, *105*, 111–12, 120, *120*, 159, *159*
free-hanging earlobes 35–36
frontal bone contour 192
frontalis muscle 91, 91, *91*, 92, *93*
frontozygomatic suture 23, 50
functional occlusial plane 166

glabella *60*, 64, *90*, 156, 172, *173*, 191, *195*
gonial outline 193
gonion *17*, 49, 52, *55*, *57*, 174, 189, *196*
gonion flare *46*, *63*, 69

hair 52, *58*, *59*, 70–1, 172, *173*, 177
*Handbook of Craniofacial Superimposition* 189–90
Hardy, Kerry May *61*
HBP (height of highest brow point) *76*, 95
height of highest brow point (HBP) *76*, 95
Hispanic characteristics *65*, *72*, 128, *129*, 189
horizontal eyelid fissure 96

incisors *28*, 47; case work 55, *58*, *61*, *63*, 66; facial comparison 189, 199–201, *200*, *202*, *203*, *203*, 205, 208; mouth 145, *146*, 148, *148*
inferior border: of ear lobe 35; of piriform aperture 193; of ramus 165, 166

inferior nasal concha 127
infraorbital foramen *57*, 149, *149*, 189
inner canthus 78, *80*
intercanine width 150, *150*
intercanthal plane 75, *76*, 94, 95
iris 75, *78*, 80, *81*, 90, 95, 157, *174*

jawline *62*, 189
Jefferson method, for reconstructing the mandible 164–173, *165*, *167*, *168*, *169*, *170*, *171*
Jones, Robert *60*
*Journal of Forensic Identification* 198
junction of roof of orbital cavity and lateral border of orbit (SOr) 166, 169, *170*

Krogman's method, for measuring the nose 103–5, 119

lacrimal fossa 75, 78–9, *79*, 82, *84*, 90, *90*, 189, 191
Lang, Rita *60*
large spread-out ears 36
lateral border: of orbit 165, 166; of orbital cavity 164; of ramus 165, 166
lateral canthus 90, 92
lateral edge of the frontalis muscle is related to the temporal fusion line *91*
lateral eyelid fold *83*
lateral part of supraorbital margin 192
lateral supraorbital rim *59*, 88, *88*, 89
Lazy Susan 14, 16, *16*, *17*, 17
lenses, camera *17*, 18, 19, 20, 21, *22*
levator anguli oris 139, *140*
levator labii superioris alaeque nasi muscle 103, *103*
life photos 7, 9, 31, 36, 37–8, 51, *51*, 55, *55*, *58*, *59*, *60*, *61*, *62*, *63*
lining up the maxillary palate 203

McGhee, David *57*
malar tubercle *23*, *24*, 45, 50, *63*, 68, 75, *78*, *80*, 180; facial comparison 189, 191, 192, *194*, *195*, 197, *201*
malocclusion 140–1, *141*, *142*

# INDEX

Manchester method, for locating the surfaces of the face 156, *156*
mandibles 5, 9, *90*, 157; case work 56, *57*, *58*, *60*, *61*, *63*, 65, *65*, 66, 69, 70, 71; face and ears 44, *46*, 48, 51, *51*, 52; facial comparison 188, 189, *196*, 197, 199, *201*, 204, 206; mouth 139, 142, *142*, 143, *144*, 145, 149, *151*; photographing the skull *16*, *17*, 17, 22, 28, *28*, 30, *30*; traumatic injury and anomalies *163*, 169, 170, 172, *173*, 174, 176, *176*, 167, *178*, 182–3
mandibular canine 44, 72, 147, *148*
mandibular outline 191
mandibular plane 166, 172
mandibular teeth 27, 44, 145, *149*, 189
masseter 139, *139*, 156
massive prominent mastoids 36
mastoid process 30, *30*, 157, *206*; case work 55, *57*, *58*, 65, 67, 69, 70, 71; face and ears 35–44, 48, 52
mastoiditis 179, *180*
maxillary bone 28, *29*, 49, 68, 145, *146*, *174*, 189, 201
maxillary canine fossa 28, 146, *147*, *194*
maxillary central incisors 55, *61*, 66, 67, 148, *148*, 158, 189, 199, *200*, *202*, *205*, 208
maxillary teeth 27, *27*, 45, 48, *60*, 105, 142, 145, 146, 189, 200, 201
May, Kerry Hardy *61*
measurements to compare the ears *206*
medial canthus 90, 92
medial eyelid 191
medial eyelid fold *80*, *84*
medial part of supraorbital margin 191
mental foramen 149, *149*
mental outline 191
mentalis 52, 139, *139*, 206, *207*
menton 165, 166
mid occlusal point: of second bicuspid 165, 166; of second molar 165, 166
midface 35, 70, 126, *140*, 191

missing mandible *58*, *65*, 163, 169, 170, 172, *173*
mixed race 9, *72*, 126–7, 180–1
modiolus 139, *139*, 156
molars *28*, 49, *58*, 144, 165, 166
Moore, Shaun *58*
mouth 139–51; UK approach to the 157–8
muscles 8, 22, 50, 70, 75, *75*, 91, 103, *103*, 139, *139*, 143–4, 156, *156*, 180–1, *205*

nasal bones 120, 159, 191
nasal cavity 44, *46*, 103, 134, *176*, 188, 189, 204
nasal opening *see* piriform aperture
nasal projection *130*, 158
nasal root 84, *84*, 85, *85*, *88*, *97*, 127
nasal sill *25*, *65*, 129, *130*, 176, 177
nasal spine 24, *24*, 159, 191, 197; case work 57, *63*, 66–8; nose 103, 104, *104*, 105, *106*, 107, 119, 132, 133–4; traumatic injury and anomalies 165, 166, 169, *170*, 171
nasalis muscle 103, *103*
nasion *60*, 191, 192; facial reconstruction in UK 156, 158, *158*, 159; nose 105, *106*, *106*, 107, 109, 112, *112*, 120, *120*; traumatic injury and anomalies 164, 166, 168, *169*
Nasion Prosthion Plane (NPP) 105, *105*, 111–12, 120, *120*, 158–9, *159*
nasolabial fold 28, *60*, *61*, *62*, 146, *147*, 147, *148*, 189
normal lens 18–19
normal occlusion 141, *141*
normal perspective 18, 21
nose 103–34; shapes, 133–4; UK approach to 158, *159*
NPP (Nasion Prosthion Plane) 105, *105*, 111–12, 120, *120*, 158–9, *159*
nuchal crest 28, *29*, *58*, *60*, *63*, 64, 67–9, 180, *180*

occlusal line 166, 191, 193
occlusion 140, *141*, *142*, 158, 189
orbicularis oculi muscle 75, *75*, 91
orbicularis oris 139, *140*

orbital cavity 5, 6, *105*, 125, 127, 149; case work 56, *61*, 67, 68, 70; eye and brow 75, 76, 77, *77*, 78, *78*, 80, 82, *82*, *85*, *91*; face and ears *38*, 43–4, 47, 48, 50, 52; facial comparison 188, 191, *194*, 204; photographing the skull 16, *17*, 24, *24*, 24, 26, *26*; traumatic injury and anomalies *164*, 165, 166, 169, *174*, 175, *176*, 177, 180
orbital structure indicating epicanthic fold *85*
outer canthus 78, *80*
overbite 72, 141, *141*, *142*

palatal plane 166
palate arch 28
palpebral fissure: height 75, *75*, *93*, 94; length 75, *75*, 93, 96
permanent retainers 182, *182*
philtrum 148, *148*, 189
photographing the skull 13–31
piriform aperture 9, 20, 24, 26, *26*, 175–7; case work , *58*, *59*, *60*, *62*, *63*, 68, 69; face and ears 47–50, *51*, 52; facial comparison 191, 192, *194*, *195*, *196*, 197; nose 103, 121, *122*, 124, 125, *125*, 126–7, *128*, 129, 130, 132, 132, 134
placement: of eyeball in orbital cavity *77*; of eyeball in skull *91*
PNS (Posterior Nasal Spine) 165, 166
pogonion 165, 166
point of focus 20
pointed lobe 40, *43*
portrait lens 21
post-bregmatic depression 180, *180*, 182
Posterior Nasal Spine (PNS) 165, 166
postmortem tooth loss 27, *28*, 57, 64, 71, 72, 143, *143*, 144, 145
Precious Jane Doe case 55
pretarsal skin crease *93*
pretarsal skin height 93, *93*
procerus muscle 75, *75*, 156
Procreate 6
Prokopec and Ubelaker method, of nasal projection *130*
prominent ears *38*

pronounced mandibular canines *148*
prosthion 105, *105*, 120, *120*
ptosis 62, 91–2, *91*

ramus 15–17, 157, 165, 166, 189
reconstruction kit, the author's *14*
rhinion *106*, 108, 158, *158*
risorius 139, *140*
Roberts, Elizabeth Ann 55
roof of orbital cavity 165, 166, 169
Rynn's method, for estimating nasal projection 104–17, *105*, *106*, *107*, *108*, *109*, *110*, **110**, *112*, *113*, *114*, *115*, *116*, *117*, *118*

s shaped brow *97*
Sassouni method, for reconstructing the mandible 164
Sculpey clay 14, *14*, 15
sella turcica inferior 165, 166
sensors, camera 18–19, 21, *22*
75% rule, for estimating mouth width 150
shutter speed 13, 19, 20, 21
skull measurements *202*, 204, *205*
skull stand 14, 16, *16*
skull to face comparison 59
skull to photo comparison 193–8, *194*, *195*, *196*, *197*, 208
skull x-rays 164, *164*, 170, *171*, 172
skull-face craniofacial superimposition *190*, *192*, *193*, *194*, *195*
small pointed lobes 40
SOr (junction of roof of orbital cavity and lateral border of orbit) 156, 169, *170*
strong brow and supraorbital margin eyebrow form *86*
strong brow and thick supraorbital rim *97*
strong brow ridge and thickened lateral supraorbital rim eyebrow form *88*
strong brow ridge and thickened lateral supraorbital rim on the skull *88*
styloid process 178, *178*

subspinale *106*, 108, 109, 113, *114*, 117, *118*, 158, *158*, 159
Sullivan, Tyler *58*
superior edge: of external auditory meatus 206, *206*; of maxillary teeth 176; of orbital cavity 23, 38, 77, 175, 204
supramastoid crest 36, 38
supraorbital cavity 83
supraorbital rim 5, 44, *59*, 75, 76, 80, 82, 86, 88, *88*, 97, *195*
symmetry 47; *see also* asymmetry

Taylor, Karen T. 4
Taylor, Dr. Kathy 5, 129
teeth 5, 27–8, *27*, *28*, 44, 47, 48, 141, *141*; in case work 55, *57*, *63*, 64, 68; loss of *see* tooth loss; mandibular 27, 43–4, 145, *148*, 189; maxillary 27, *27*, 44, 48, *60*, 105, 142, 145, 146, 189, 200, 201; roots of *27*, 28
telephoto lenses 18, 20
temporal bones 36
temporal fusion line 91, *91*
temporal line 191, 192
thickened lateral supraorbital rims *59*, *88*
3D modelling software 155
tissue depth 156–9, *156*, *158*, *159*
tissue depth markers 35, *57*, *81*, 150, *151*, 156, *156*, *174*, 203; nose 103, 105, *106*, 107, 108, 109, 111–112, 113, 114, *115*, 116, *118*; photographing the skull 13, 15, 17, 18, 22, 25
tooth loss 26, *28*, 44, 143–5, *143*, *144*, 177, *196*, 204; case work 57, 64, 71, 72
torus 178

trapezius muscle 28, 180
traumatic injury 163–183
triangle 16, *16*
triangular brow 97
two-tangent method, for measuring the nose 118–19, *119*, 159

underbite 141, *141*, 142, *142*, 177
uneven ears 39, *39*, 206
United Kingdom facial reconstruction 155–9

vertical and horizontal guides (lines) at specific locations 46
vomer 25, 103

Wacom Cintiq drawing tablet *6*
weak brow: and high nasal root 97; and low nasal root 97
weak brow ridge: and high nasal root eyebrow form *88*; and low nasal root eyebrow form *86*; and low nasal root on skull *86*
Whitnall's tubercle 24, *24*, 50, *63*, 68, 75, 78, *78*, 180; facial comparison 189, 191, 192, *194*, *195*, 197, *201*
wide angle lenses 18
Wilkinson, Caroline 4, 80, *81*, 86, 143, 145, 146

x-rays, of skull 164, *164*, 170, *171*, 172

zoom lenses 19, 21
zygomatic arches 28, *29*, 191
zygomatic bones 28, *58*, *60*, *62*, *63*, 70, 71, *201*, 204, *205*
zygomatic major 139, *140*
zygomatic minor 139, *140*